But Not Today

But Not Today

My Journey through Brain Cancer

Doree O'Connell

Copyright © 2019 by Doree O'Connell.

Library of Congress Control Number: 2019901005
ISBN: Hardcover 978-1-7960-1266-8
Softcover 978-1-7960-1265-1
eBook 978-1-7960-1264-4

All rights reserved. No part of this book may be reproduced or transmitted in any form or by any means, electronic or mechanical, including photocopying, recording, or by any information storage and retrieval system, without permission in writing from the copyright owner.

Any people depicted in stock imagery provided by Getty Images are models, and such images are being used for illustrative purposes only.
Certain stock imagery © Getty Images.

Print information available on the last page.

Rev. date: 02/08/2019

To order additional copies of this book, contact:
Xlibris
1-888-795-4274
www.Xlibris.com
Orders@Xlibris.com
788446

DEDICATION

To my daughter, Jennifer,
my greatest teacher in life,

and to my life partner, Jack,
who makes me laugh.

All proceeds from the sale of this book will be donated to help fund brain tumor research at
UCSF Brain Tumor Center
505 Parnassus Avenue
Department of Neurosurgery, M786
San Francisco, CA 94143

ACKNOWLEDGMENTS

Cancer is a solitary journey. No one experienced my unspoken dread that my brain would never work as it had before; no one could go through treatment for me; no one felt my financial worry. Yet cancer is also a journey one cannot travel alone. I was surrounded by love and acceptance and knew that at each step in the process, if I asked, someone would help.

I am grateful that fate sent me to Dr. Mitchel Berger, for I believe without his brilliance and steady hands, without the supporting cast of nurses and technicians at the University of California at San Francisco Medical Center, and without the follow-up care of Dr. Susan Chang, I'd be a statistic today.

I am grateful for those I met on this journey and who have gone on ahead: Marilyn, Pauline, Chris, Don, Terry, and Ann, I wouldn't be who I am today without the life lessons of courage, hope, and faith that you taught me.

I am grateful for family and friends, whose calls and visits lifted me from a sense of isolation and engaged me in the daily activities of life.

And I am grateful to my writers group: Pat, Sue, Jennifer, Linda, Dottie, Marilyn, Anna, Mary, and Bill, thank you. You threatened and cajoled me to finish this story, and you listened to every single word and more. I love you all.

CONTENTS

Dedication v
Acknowledgments vii
Foreword xi
The MRI xiii
Introduction xv

1   Evening, Tuesday, April 4, 2006 1
2   A Job for Italy
    October 2005 3
3   The Downward Slide
    October 2005 8
4   Foreshadowing
    March 31, 2006 13
5   Heartbeat in My Head
    Sunday, April 2, 2006 18
6   French Hospital Emergency Room
    Dawn, Tuesday, April 4, 2006 25
7   Dawn Patrol 28
8   A Shadow in My Brain
    Early Morning, Tuesday, April 4, 2006 33
9   Sierra Vista Hospital
    Midmorning, Tuesday, April 4, 2006 36
10 Ambulance Ride to UCSF
    Evening, Tuesday, April 4, 2006 41
11 UCSF and Dr. Berger
    Early, Wednesday, April 5, 2006 47
12 A Day of Tests
    Wednesday, April 5, 2006 53
13 Brain Surgery
    Dawn, Thursday, April 6, 2006 59

14 Surgery Report and Pathology Report
   April 6, 2006 64
15 Recovery Room
   Nighttime, Thursday, April 6, 2006 67
16 First Day of the Rest of My Life
   Friday, April 7, 2006 73
17 Out!
   Sunday, April 9, 2006 79
18 Discharge Summary
   April 9, 2006 83
19 Home
   Monday, April 10, 2006 86
20 Dr. Chang's Diagnosis
   Wednesday, April 19, 2006 91
21 Fifty with a Vengeance
   Thursday, April 20, 2006 95
22 The Low Point
   Saturday, April 29, 2006 100
23 Dr. Stella
   Wednesday, May 3, 2006 104
24 Radiation and the Mask
   Friday, May 5, 2006 111
25 Chemotherapy and Dr. Spillane
   Tuesday, July 18, 2006 116
26 California Department of Education
   September 2006 120
27 Nutritional Advice 123
28 UCSF Medical Center: MRI Report and Letter
   March 9, 2007 126
29 Financial Issues 130
30 Italy!
   April 2007 133

Epilogue: Another Tumor – May 2016 137
The Final Chapter – Today 141

FOREWORD

I will never forget the day I met Doree. She had just been transferred to the Neurosurgery Service at UCSF after being diagnosed with a brain tumor. I expected to find someone so shaken by the diagnosis that I would have to wait until her husband, Jack, arrived to review the plan and chart a management course. Yet Doree was calm and collected and, although visibly concerned about the uncertainty of her future, she approached me with full confidence and merely stated that she understood the situation and wanted to move forward and take care of this. I told her I would call Jack, who was driving up from the Central Coast, and reassure him that she would be fine.

    The surgery went well, and Doree began her long journey of treatment and care. She would come to see myself and Dr. Susan Chang, chief of Neuro-Oncology, at UCSF. Doree always came with a smile on her face. She never asked the dreaded question, "Why me?" Instead, she asked if she could help with any other patients who were struggling with their diagnosis. She was always motivated to stay positive and live life to the fullest.

    I cannot help but think that her ever-present smile, positive attitude, and outlook resulted in her prolonged survival. In fact, she is one of only a handful of patients who have lived beyond ten years with her diagnosis. We were all devastated when Doree developed a recurrence; I knew this would be difficult to overcome. Yet Doree's positive attitude and desire to beat the tumor kept us so encouraged and motivated to help her. She fought valiantly until the very end and always had a smile on her face.

I will never forget Doree and her husband and daughter, Jack and Jen. They were magnificent throughout the entire time and were the very best of what families and caregivers should be during something like this. Doree will always give me inspiration and hope. She will always give me the strength to get up yet another day and fight this battle with someone else. She will always be with me, forever and a day.

>Mitchel S. Berger, MD
>Chair, Department of Neurological Surgery
>University of California, San Francisco

THE MRI

Hospital gown worn backwards
as a makeshift robe covers
one-size-fits-all pants and open-backed top.
Rubber-grip socks stick
to slick tile floors as I follow the technician
to the imaging room.

I've done this before, I tell her. Can we
skip the tape?
I promise to keep my head still
without it. She smiles
and tapes my head to the table anyway.

Hands pinned under hips keep them
on the narrow metal bed. Rolled in
head first, eyes closed, I can't see
the machine that entombs me.
I feel it, though, and rest my arms
against cold metal sides.
Okay, Hon? she asks as she pats my toes.

Jackhammers pound through earplugs
and cloth pads wedged between my head
and the cool smooth tube.

I feel sound deep in my core
where it clacks and thrums.
I conjure sunshine, rivers, expanses of tropical sea
but can't outrun my mind,
wonder instead if she can see thoughts of sadness
or worry. I construct
a grocery list in my head,
plan where we'll lunch on the drive home,
visualize health.

The blasts stop. I fret,
imagine her poring over scans,
imagine the worst.
I clear throat and wiggle toes to remind her
I'm still here.
Steady hands roll out the table. An IV
pricks my arm, and
as cool dye flows through veins, I taste
a faint aroma of metal
and alcohol.
Okay, Hon? she asks and pats my toes.
I offer a thumbs-up as I squeeze back into
the narrow tube.

When I leave, I ask the receptionist
to cut off my wristband.
I avoid the elevator,
climb four flights of stairs,
and relish deep breaths of
cold San Francisco air.

INTRODUCTION

I read somewhere on one of those websites—the ones that brain cancer patients should avoid at all costs—that the life expectancy of a person facing glioblastoma multiforme (GBM) averages nine to fourteen months. Well, it has been ten years since my GBM diagnosis. That means I've had ten years of family and friends, of joy and laughter, of life's bittersweet moments, and I know I am truly blessed.

My tale is a snapshot in time: childhood flashbacks intermixed with medical jargon within the frame of a planned trip to Italy in 2006 and the actual trip in April 2007, one year after my diagnosis. I offer my personal story of surviving malignant brain cancer as a story of hope, something I search for in every book, article, or website I read, even today. We brain cancer survivors learn to accept and embrace our altered lives with spirit and joy and a keen understanding that what we are left with at the end are our words, our actions, our memories, and the hope that—if we're lucky—our lives have mattered.

I have learned that attitude is everything, that my thoughts are the energy that steer my life, that laughter is better than medicine, that hope is forever.

CHAPTER ONE

Evening, Tuesday, April 4, 2006

"What's the plan?" I ask.

"Still stormy," my husband, Jack, answers. "We've been waiting to see if the medevac plane can fly, but with the storm it's too risky. You're going by ambulance."

"To San Francisco?"

"To UCSF. Jen and I will follow in the morning."

I grab the hand of my nineteen-year-old daughter, Jennifer, as I'm wheeled past her. "I'll be okay," I say. She squeezes my hand and nods.

At the door of the emergency room I am shifted to the gurney and rolled to the waiting ambulance. I see rain illuminated against light posts and streaking against windows, hear the rat-a-tat as it pounds the pavement.

An attendant jumps into the back and guides the gurney along one side of the ambulance, where it is fastened to the floor. The gurney is narrow, and I grip the edges, fearful of rolling off during the four-hour trip, until the attendant reaches across me and straps me in at several points.

"Okay?" he asks. At my nod he taps the window that separates the back from the cab, then straps himself in on a jump seat across from me. He reaches for my wrist and counts the beats of my pulse, then checks the IV bag that is suspended above me before he speaks again. "How do you feel?"

"Okay." I close my eyes. "Thank you. Long night for you."

"We've been on hold, waiting to see what happens with the weather." He pauses, then asks bluntly, "What's wrong with you?"

I open my eyes to study him. The puzzlement etched on his youthful face is clear. I answer him simply: "Brain tumor."

I think about my path to this point, about how this journey started, and I know that to tell my story properly, I need to go back to the beginning.

CHAPTER TWO

A Job for Italy
October 2005

"I want to go to Italy." My announcement comes without warning and swirls amid dust motes caught in shafts of sunlight streaming through high living room windows. Beams angle across a brown couch with scattered pillows of muted paisley and rest against my husband's lanky frame. In the light, I can see strands of gray in his brown hair.

Jack looks up from the Sunday paper, his brown eyes startled. "What?" he asks.

"Italy," I repeat. "Are you at all interested?"

"Italy?" Jack resumes reading the newspaper. "Not at all."

"It's the place I most want to see." I hesitate before adding, "You know, I almost went to Europe after high school. I never got the chance in college. We got married instead."

Jack lowers the paper again. "You're serious."

"I am."

"Can you find someone else to go with you?"

"I can. You don't mind?" I think of the long weeks my husband works and his years commuting from our home on the Central Coast of California to the state capital, Sacramento. These days, his idea of a vacation is a week at home with no airplane rides. I feel a twinge of

3

guilt. "This is my version of a clock ticking. I know I told you I wanted to go to Europe before I was fifty."

"Then go." Jack grins. "As long as I don't have to go with you. Who do you have in mind?"

"My friend Cheryl. She's going next summer, asked if I want to go with her."

"Summer?"

"Well, in May."

"You'll already be fifty."

"Close enough. Do you think you'll ever get to Europe?"

"Yeah, I do. I've got one good trip in me. It'll just have to wait until I'm done with this job. As long as we go to a country where I can find things to eat, I'll go with you then."

I laugh, understanding his penchant for plain American food, then am thoughtful for a few minutes. "I need a job," I finally say.

Jack again lowers the newspaper. "What?"

"A job."

"Teaching?"

"I don't think so." My smile is sad. Ten years earlier, after twenty years as a court reporter, I'd returned to college to finish the degree I'd interrupted when Jack and I married. I enjoyed being a student again, so much so that after earning my degree in English, I stayed in school an additional year to obtain my teaching credential. After all, that's the direction I was headed when I left school at twenty to marry.

Only problem was that teaching wasn't a natural fit, at least not in the elementary grades I chose to teach. As a student teacher, I felt lost in the first-grade classroom I was assigned, never knowing if my students were learning to read because of my hard work, or despite it.

I had better success in my next assignment, a sixth-grade classroom of lower-income students. I was unable to speak more than a few Spanish words when I communicated with the students' parents, but I clicked with the thirty-four energetic and boisterous twelve-year-olds in my class. Finally, I thought. Whew. They sure taught me a whole lot about perseverance and patience. I smiled to myself and thought about those students: Santos, Jaime, Maya, Lupe, Alejandro, Eddie, Erma . . .

Erma. Erma was my most vocal critic. My first few weeks in class were marked by confrontations with her. She corrected my mispronunciations and argued over math answers, her dissents all marked by flashing black eyes in an unsmiling face. When Erma conducted loud conversations in Spanish, I was her favorite topic. I understood just enough.

Maya noticed. "Mrs. O'Connell, do you know Spanish?"

"Hmm," I answered. "I should tell you that I really do like my skirt."

Maya gasped, not knowing that I had recognized only three words in Erma's last diatribe. Erma remained unapologetic.

Another student, Lupe, stayed in one day at lunch. "Mrs. O'Connell, can I tell you about my crush?"

"Of course," I answered.

"Oh, Mrs. O'Connell, he doesn't even know I exist. I tried to talk to him at recess, but he just went off with Danny. So I passed him a note in class—" She stopped, guilty.

I patted her shoulder. "I know. I saw." Santos had put the note, unopened, in his desk, and the sudden sheen of tears in Lupe's eyes had kept me silent.

"I think I'm too fat," Lupe said and covered her face.

I put my arm around her. "You are not. You're a beautiful girl. It's not you." Lupe's expression was comical, a mixture of hope and angst, but I allowed myself only a tiny smile. "Girls your age are interested in boys. That's normal. Boys, though, are clueless. They are not ready for girls, and there's nothing you can do to change that." I thought for a moment. "Santos plays softball every day, doesn't he?"

Lupe wiped her eyes.

"And you're an excellent ballplayer, aren't you?"

She looked up, curious.

"So here's what you do: you play softball. Play on his team every day. Be patient. He'll notice you." I gave Lupe an extra squeeze and pushed her out the door.

When the last bell rang a few days later, the students shoved books in backpacks and raced outside, all except Eddie. He lifted the lid to his desk and tidied its contents: books in a stack on the left, papers on the right, pencils up front in a neat row. His brown eyes under a mop of curly black hair watched me over the top of his desk. His customary happy-go-lucky smile was missing.

"Any big after-school plans, Eddie?" I asked.

Eddie hesitated. "Well, I like to be home at four so I can watch *Emeril*."

I stopped pushing in desk chairs and straightened, surprised. It wasn't what I expected to hear. "Can you cook, Eddie?"

"Yeah."

"That's a real talent."

Eddie sat tall, pleased by my response. "Yeah. I like Emeril. He's cool."

"What do you cook?"

"Everything," he answered.

I laughed. "What's your favorite thing to cook?" I listened for a long time as Eddie recited favorite recipes, told me how to keep a soufflé from falling, and explained four different ways to cook a Thanksgiving turkey.

"And that's why I don't do good in school, Mrs. O'Connell. I don't want to read *The Sign of the Beaver* or *Bridge to Terabithia*. I'd rather read cookbooks. And I'm terrible in math, but why do I need it if I'm gonna be a chef?"

And there it was, the reason for the conversation: Eddie's struggle with math. "How much vanilla do you put in a batch of oatmeal cookies?" I asked.

"A teaspoon."

"How about flour?"

"Two cups, and two cups of oatmeal."

"What if you're not very hungry and only want to bake half a batch of cookies?"

"You cut all the ingredients in half."

"So half a teaspoon of vanilla—" I started.

Eddie finished my sentence. "—and one cup of flour and one cup of oatmeal."

"Let's say you own a big catering company. Your oatmeal cookie recipe makes five dozen cookies." I paused. "Let's also say you are expecting 120 people at the party. What do you do?"

Eddie thought for a moment. "Well, five dozen is sixty cookies, because that's five times twelve. I have to make two batches."

"You've just done math, Eddie. What if you want everybody to be able to eat four cookies? You know how to figure that out because you know math."

"But I'm not good in math."

"Yes, you are. You just proved it." I had an idea. "Let's work together after school. We can make up cooking problems." When Eddie hesitated, I added, "And I'll be sure you're home by four o'clock."

Over time, my rapport with the students grew. Jaime confided he was tired because he had helped his dad pick crops all weekend. Alejandro told me about the *curandera* his mother consulted when his younger brother was sick. Danny and I devised a plan to keep him caught up on schoolwork when he spent a month with his family in Mexico. And Nina picked me to be on her softball team. "Only if Erma can be my base runner," I said, ignoring Erma's sudden stillness. "She's fast."

Before I even saw the end coming, my last day in sixth grade had arrived. The day was emotional and heartfelt: thirty-four hugs, thirty-four handwritten letters left in a pile on my desk. Erma's was the only letter in an envelope addressed to me in decorative, flowery cursive. She hesitated as she left it on top of the stack, then snatched it away.

"No, Mrs. O'Connell," she said. "I want to read it to you."

And she did, I remembered. Erma, my most vocal champion.

Jack's voice broke through my reverie. "A job," he repeated. "Why?"

"For Italy," I answered. "To pay my way. I want to go. I'll start looking today."

CHAPTER THREE

The Downward Slide
October 2005

"I'm starting to get excited," I tell Cheryl. I burrow deeper into the jacket zipped to my chin, my cheeks red from the stiff ocean breeze blowing across Pismo Beach, a town ten miles from my home.

Cheryl, her long blond hair clipped back, keeps pace in the sand with me as we lean into the wind. "Are you dreaming in Italian yet?" she asks, knowing that I drive around town with my Italian language CDs in the car.

"Ask me something about the days of the week or the weather." I laugh. "I'm not sure how far that will get us. *Buon pomeriggio. Fa freddo oggi. Piove e ventoso.* The CD with food names comes next. Now those will be valuable words to know."

"We need to think about an itinerary. When does your job start?"

"Next week." I pull the collar of my jacket up to my ears and tuck short, wavy hair in the back, which lasts only until the next gust of wind. "It's perfect. Cal Poly is going to let me work three long days a week on Tuesdays, Wednesdays, and Thursdays," I say, referring to the state university about four miles from my home in San Luis Obispo. "And the job runs through March, so I can get myself ready in April—"

"—to go in May," Cheryl finishes. "I've been reading guidebooks. I know a few places I want to visit because I missed them last time."

"Well, I'm a good person to travel with. I haven't seen a thing."

"Get ready to be amazed. I think we should book our tickets sooner rather than later. Once we have the dates, it will be easier to plan the trip."

"I've got about a million United Airlines miles," I say. "I'd like to use them. Hey, when we're done with our walk, come over and we'll check flight schedules online."

"Now that," Cheryl says, "is a plan."

~~~

I spend my free moments the next few months poring over travel books and memorizing maps. I collect train schedules and hotel recommendations from guidebooks and Italian tourism websites and check currency exchange rates daily. Three weeks is longer than any trip I've ever taken. Still, fitting everything I want to experience in that time frame will be tricky. Faraway places I have only read about fill my dreams: Rome, with its Colosseum and history of ancient times; Ponte Vecchio and Michelangelo's David in Florence; Siena's tile roofs, narrow cobblestone passageways, and Il Campo. All would soon be a reality, an experience I have waited a lifetime to see.

One evening in early March, Cheryl calls. "Are you up for a beach walk tomorrow, maybe nine o'clock? I've got an idea of what our itinerary should be, and I want to run it by you. We have to start thinking about reserving rooms."

I'm quiet for a long moment. "Are you there?" Cheryl asks.

"Oh, yeah. Sorry. I'm looking at my calendar." I drag myself off the couch where I've been resting and shuffle into the kitchen. "Looks clear," I say.

"How about I drive? I think it's my turn."

"Great. I'll be ready for you." I hang up the phone and shuffle back to the couch. I'm just tired, I think. I'll go to bed early, and that ocean air will do wonders.

~~~

The morning still has wisps of fog lying against the Central Coast hills that rim Pismo Beach. Cool air holds a promise of sun's warmth;

sand, smooth and damp from the early morning high tide, crunches beneath our feet. Cheryl talks; I listen.

"Are you feeling all right?" Cheryl finally asks.

"I think I'm fighting off something," I answer. "Either that, or I'm stressed by work. Isn't that sad? I used to be able to work long hours like that."

"Well, you're in a new position with new people and new demands. I think feeling some sort of stress is normal."

"Maybe I should've spread thirty hours a week over four days instead of three. Maybe I'm just wearing myself out." I shrug. "I'll be fine." I stop to point to the sky. "Pelicans."

"At least a dozen." Cheryl stands beside me, and her neck cranes to follow the birds' arrow-formation flight overhead. "Spectacular."

"Aren't they?" I gesture to a patch of white sand. "Do you mind if we just sit and talk today? I want to hear your ideas. And then I'll tell you what I've been reading."

"About—"

"Italia." I smile. "The land of my ancestors."

As Cheryl outlines the route she wants to follow, I idly watch two girls fill colorful plastic buckets with sand at water's edge. Sisters, I decide, remembering a time when my sister Leslee and I had done much the same thing.

That particular day, Leslee had begged me to help her make a sand castle. "Please?" she asked.

"Okay," I said. "If we're going to make a sand castle, it has to be a real castle. Fill up these buckets."

Leslee jumped up. "A castle for a princess," she said, and scurried to follow orders.

We set to work building a castle fit for royalty, crafting and sculpting until the encroaching tide sent us scuttling for cover.

"Wave!" Leslee shrieked.

I grabbed the buckets and scrambled for safety as fast as my eight-year-old legs could carry me, but in my hurry, I mowed down Leslee, and we sprawled in the sand. We craned our necks to peer down the length of beach that moments before had been our playground. Together we watched the castle's moat fill with seawater until the walls collapsed and the seaweed flags and driftwood drawbridge sank into a sandy mush, then floated away with the tide.

"Poor princess," Leslee said, and we lay in the sand and giggled.

Cheryl's voice brought me back to the present with a start. "So what do you think?"

"I think, since you've been to Italy before, we should be sure to see the places you want to see. I know you've been to Florence and Rome, but I'd like to spend a couple days in each city. And then I want to see Siena, and I'd like to hike the trail between the villages of Cinque Terre."

"Me too. And Florence and Rome are worth seeing again."

"Other than that, I'm happy to let you decide how we do the trip. My guidebook is in the car. I'll show you a couple accommodations I flagged, and then we should send some emails to ask about availability."

"Wonderful." Cheryl jumps up. "Let's go. Are you still done with work at the end of March?"

I climb slowly to my feet. "Well, they've asked if I'd stay longer, so I think I'm going to work through mid-April. I'm telling myself it's more money for Italy."

Cheryl nods.

"But did I tell you they asked if I'd come back after our trip?"

"Really? Full time?"

I nod.

"What'd you tell them?"

"I said I'd let them know." I hesitate. "I like everybody I work with. I love the students. I'm honored they asked. It's just that—" I stop and point to my head. "Maybe the building I'm working in is giving me these headaches. It's an old office building. They're building a new one."

"Maybe you're just putting too much pressure on yourself," Cheryl says.

"Maybe. I lost my keys at work this week. I stopped at Campus Market to buy coffee on my way to the office, and when I got there, I couldn't unlock the door. I couldn't find my keys, and I distinctly remembered picking them up from the kitchen counter at home to bring to work."

"What happened?"

"I retraced my steps, started from the beginning of my morning. I searched the car, stopped at Campus Market and asked if anyone turned in keys, then followed the path back to the office. Fortunately, by then someone else had arrived, so the office door was unlocked. My boss said to go get more keys made. By lunchtime, I convinced myself I had imagined I'd picked up the keys off the counter, that they were actually sitting where I left them at home. And then I got my lunch out of the refrigerator."

"Oh no."

"Yup. Nice and cold. And I have no memory of putting them in the lunch bag."

"Anyone can do that," Cheryl says. "Sounds like something I'd do when I'm trying to do too much at once."

"That must be it. I need to slow down. Nobody remembers how fast you get things done, but they sure remember when you do something goofy like that." I grimace. "Maybe I should just quit now and not work the extra weeks. Save face."

"Well," Cheryl says, "if it's meant to be, it will happen. Now, let's check out those Italian hotels."

CHAPTER FOUR

Foreshadowing
March 31, 2006

"I fell at work today." I set the frying pan on the stove, add olive oil, and turn on the burner.

Jack looks up from where he sits on the couch in front of the evening news and frowns, the edges of his brown eyes crinkling with concern. "In the office?"

"No. I was outside, walking across campus to deliver a document to another department."

"Hurt yourself?"

I toss red peppers, broccoli, and onions in the sizzling olive oil, then cover the vegetables with a lid before I turn back to Jack and shrug. "No. What is it you always say, that I'm the only person you know who can fall up stairs?"

"You fell up stairs?"

"Actually, I tripped up a curb and fell flat. And then I hopped right up, made sure there were no students walking near me."

A smile tugs the corner of Jack's mouth. "That sounds like you. You okay?"

"Yeah. Just my pride." I pause for a moment before adding, "You know, something about my foot didn't feel right, like I couldn't lift my foot."

"How do you mean?"

"Just that. Like my ankle wouldn't bend, or I couldn't point my toes up. I can't describe it any better than that."

"How about now?"

I flex my right foot. "Stiff. Maybe I bruised it."

"How many more days left at the job?"

"Well, I finished the contract yesterday. I worked an extra day today to help the staff get organized for the first day of spring quarter. I'm still debating whether I want to work through mid-April, but I told them I'd be there at least next week. I need to make a decision, let them know." I shift my weight to again flex my right foot. I raise the pan's lid to stir vegetables with the spatula, then replace the lid before turning back to Jack. My husband's attention is focused on the TV. Sports news is on, and Major League Baseball scores catch his interest.

I sigh and pull down the oven door to check the chicken. Almost done. I take dinner plates from the counter and set them on the narrow kitchen table. Only two for dinner tonight; our nineteen-year-old daughter, Jennifer, is visiting friends in Los Angeles this weekend and won't return until Monday.

"Almost ready?" Jack's voice drifts across the kitchen.

"Almost." I open a cupboard door and grab two glasses, but one slips seamlessly through my grasp and shatters on the hard tile floor.

"Hold on," Jack orders. "I'll get the broom. Don't move."

I clutch the second glass with both hands and carefully set it on the kitchen counter. The accident has been swift, the sound of splintering glass startling. I stand still and absent-mindedly rub a trembling hand across my forehead.

Jack straightens, balancing a dustpan of glass pieces. "I think I got it all."

"What a klutz," I say, massaging my forehead.

Jack dumps the glass shards into the trash can under the kitchen sink. "You feel okay?"

"I think I'm just tired. I've had this headache all week. Maybe I am getting sick."

"Probably nothing a good night's sleep won't cure."

"That," I agree, "sounds wonderful."

~~~

Saturday dawns, the day bright and clear as only spring days near the California coast can be. No dampness, no fog drifts through the verdant valley rimmed with ancient volcanic peaks. I lie in bed and listen to the sounds of Jack fixing his breakfast. I hear him open the front door and moments later hear the thud of two morning papers dropped on the carpet near the couch. A kitchen cupboard closes, metal jangles, and measured steps follow excited panting and scrabbling paws across the tile foyer floor. The front door closes quietly. Jack and Missy, our golden retriever, are going to the park.

I add another pillow to the stack already propped behind my neck until I recline in a half-sitting position. I close my eyes and breathe the peace of the room. I doze fitfully and awaken with the sound of an opened door, the lapping of water from the thirsty dog's water bucket, then later by the rustle of newspapers. These are familiar noises, the kinds that fill a home with gentle comfort and a sense of belonging. But today the noises compete with the sound of the heartbeat pounding in my head. Waves, I think. I hear waves crashing against a rocky shore. The sound expands until it pushes against my head, like an overfilled balloon stretched to the point of bursting. I listen to the noises in my head until, rocked by the rhythm, I sleep.

Weekends are golden in the O'Connell household. Jack's position as superintendent of all public K–12 schools in California finds him often on the road to visit school sites, where he holds difficult budget conversations with school principals, meets with teachers to learn best practices, or participates in awards ceremonies for deserving students. When he isn't traveling, Jack convenes with his deputy directors who oversee 1,400 state employees in the six-story Department of Education building in downtown Sacramento. He meets with visiting school board members, discusses education legislation with legislative staff from the state capitol building across the street, and attends bimonthly board hearings for the State Board of Education, University of California Regents, and California State University Trustees, often working late only to leave the building in time to attend an evening function. I occasionally meet Jack at a conference in Los Angeles or drive to Sacramento to spend a few days with him, but he makes every effort to be home in San Luis Obispo on weekends. So when Jack enters our bedroom in search of his swim trunks with a plan to go to the club for a swim and workout, I go with him.

"You're not swimming much," Jack says later as he stops after several laps to catch his breath. "You still not feeling well?"

I remove my goggles and turn to place them behind me on the pool deck. "Still have a headache. These goggles hurt, I think from pressure in my head. The cap does too." I pull the blue silicone cap from my head, set it next to the goggles, and dunk my head underwater. "Maybe I'll use the kickboard a little."

"Or just get out."

"Maybe." I massage my temples. "Maybe the hot tub sounds better today."

Jack strokes down the lane. I rub my hand across my forehead and debate what to do. By the time Jack returns to my end of the pool, I have decided. "I'll be in the hot tub," I say. Jack lifts one hand in acknowledgment as he turns to swim another lap.

I dry myself with hands that seem to belong to another, as if someone from a great distance has reached out to help me with my task. I wrap the striped beach towel across my chest and tuck in the ends, then turn to collect my belongings. My goggles and swim cap lie alongside swim fins and kickboard at pool's edge. I pick up my goggles, then my cap. When I reach for the fins, I notice goggles still on the deck. That's funny, I think. I know I picked those up. I bend again to retrieve my goggles, and one swim fin slips from my grasp. I set the goggles and cap on the ground, tuck the kickboard under my arm, and grip both fins. But when I bend to pick up the goggles and cap, the kickboard drops to the ground, and when I reach for that, the goggles fall from my hand. I concentrate on one item at a time and finally tuck each individually into my swim bag, so focused on my task I do not notice the amused smiles from sunbathers near me.

"I'm going to the hot tub," I remind Jack when he next surfaces for air. "And then I'll shower and meet you in the car. Take your time."

An hour later, my head still pulses and roars as I rest it against the seat back. Jack opens the passenger door, stows his towel and jacket in the back seat, and sits next to me. "Want me to drive?"

I shake my head. "I can." I start the car, turn to look over my shoulder to see what's behind me before I back out of the parking space, but instead shift the car into drive and start forward. I brake and sheepishly glance at Jack. It's too much to hope he hasn't noticed my error. "Oops," I say, and put the car into reverse. "Getting a little ahead of myself."

Jack's cell phone rings, and he answers it. As he talks, I clutch the wheel with both hands, point the car down the street, and gingerly head for home.

CHAPTER FIVE

Heartbeat in My Head
Sunday, April 2, 2006

Sunday is another day at the athletic club. Jack swims laps and uses the weight room equipment. I find a kickboard and begin to kick laps, but my energy soon flags. I get out of the pool, sink into a lounge chair, and doze poolside in the shade.

At home later that evening, I sit at my desk and stare at a stack of mail. When Jack's career change years ago sent him on weekly road trips to Sacramento and other cities throughout the state, I assumed more of the home responsibilities. Tomorrow's the third, I think. Better tackle the bills. For a long while I am unable to direct my hands to follow my thoughts. Eventually, though, and with a stubborn concentration, I sort through the mail and separate bills from obvious junk mail and grocery store flyers that I stuff into the recycling bin at my feet. Next, I focus my attention on the collection of bills and will my hands to reach for them. I clutch an envelope in my left hand and slide my right forefinger inside the sealed flap to open it, but my right hand seems without strength, and my fingers refuse to obey. I switch hands and press the envelope against the desk with the side of my right hand to hold it still and slide my left forefinger under the gummed flap to open it. That works, I think. I'll do it that way. Slowly, the bills waiting for a check to be written and stuffed into a return envelope are shuffled into a semblance of order.

Darn migraine. At least I think it's a migraine. I paw through loose papers on my desk with numb fingers and hands that feel too stiff to belong to me. Where's my checkbook? I look down, realize that I hold it in my hand but can't feel it. Maybe it's hormones, I think. Fifty hits hard.

As evening wears on, I struggle to line up the dollar amounts I log in my checkbook. In frustration, I slash a horizontal line across the page to begin my column of figures time and again, but each successive effort proves more difficult than the previous one. I lay aside my pen. Maybe I'll just write the checks that I know are due and figure out the checkbook when I feel better. Soon I have a collection of six or seven envelopes with payments sealed inside. I pull stamps and address labels from the top desk drawer and affix them to the envelopes, finishing just as Jack rounds the corner.

"I took Missy outside," he says. "I'm going upstairs to pack for the week. I've got an early flight tomorrow. Can you set the alarm for 5:15?"

I groan. "I'd better get to bed too."

The sky is still dark when I wake. I watch Jack through half-opened eyes. Early Monday mornings have been a part of our routine for almost thirty years. He showers, shaves, and dons his suit, all with an economy of motion. Necktie in hand, he grabs his bag and heads down the stairs. I know this is the signal for me to throw back the bedcovers, grope for sweatshirt and sweatpants, shove my feet into a pair of clogs, and meet him at the car.

"What do you have going on today?" Jack asks as he knots his tie at the downstairs bathroom mirror. He straightens his collar, smoothes down his tie the length of his blue dress shirt, and checks where the tip ends at his belt.

"Nothing scheduled. Jennifer will be home tonight, but other than that no work today." I sigh and answer his unspoken question. "Yeah,

I've got to kick this, whatever it is." I place my palms against the sides of my head and massage my temples, with no relief. "I can hear my heartbeat pounding in my head."

"At least we know you're alive." Jack picks up his bag, collects his briefcase and his airplane boarding pass, and heads to the garage. "Ready when you are," he says.

∼∼∼

I spend the day in bed, pillows stacked behind my head and shoulders. The sound of crashing surf pounds my senses and interrupts fitful sleep. I watch the clock, noting every hour as it passes, yet time is meaningless. In late afternoon, when the sound of the garage door opening breaks through the throb in my head, I struggle to sit up.

"Hi, Mom," Jennifer calls up the stairs. "I'm home."

"Hi, honey." I shuffle to the top of the stairs to peer down at my daughter. "How was the drive?"

"Good. I left L.A. at noon, so not much traffic."

"There's always traffic in L.A."

"Well, not much traffic for L.A., then."

I pause on my descent down the staircase to smile at my daughter. "How's Kim?"

"Kim's great. It was so good to see her. I miss her." Jennifer, suitcase dragging behind her, passes me on the stairway. "We went out to breakfast before I left, but that was a long time ago and I'm starving. Do we have any food?"

I frown and rub my forehead. "No leftovers, I don't think. How about some pasta?"

"Yum. I'll be down."

I shuffle into the kitchen, find a pan to fill with water, and place it on a burner. I open a cupboard, study my choices, and select whole-wheat fettuccini and a jar of spaghetti sauce. The pan I select is too small for the long strands of dried pasta, so I break the fettuccine in half before dropping them into boiling water and watch as softened lengths of pasta sink beneath the foamy surface.

"You and Dad have a good weekend?" Jennifer's voice at my elbow makes me jump.

"Pretty good."

"What'd you do?"

"The usual. Went swimming, did things around the house." I rub cool hands across my forehead, then smooth them through my unruly dark blond hair where I let them rest against my scalp.

"Is this a new look?" Jennifer eyes my floppy sweats and disheveled appearance.

"You noticed." I muster a smile. I stir the pasta, replace the pan lid, and lower the flame under the pan before turning back to my daughter. "I haven't felt well this weekend. In fact, this whole week."

"You're sick? What's wrong?"

I shrug. "Wish I knew. As near as I can tell, I've got a migraine."

"Have you ever had one before?"

"I must not have. I don't think so. It must be hormones."

"Hormones?"

"The doctor put me on birth control pills last month, trying to ease me into menopause. I must be having a reaction to them."

Jennifer is matter-of-fact. "Call her."

"I should." I put the strainer in the sink, lift the pan from the stovetop, and drain the pasta water. I set the pan back on the stove and reach for the jar of sauce. "Can you do this?" I ask, sliding the jar across the counter to Jennifer.

Jennifer pops the lid off with a flick of her wrist and pushes the jar back. I grasp the jar with both hands and carefully pour out half. I set the jar on the counter, clutch my spoon with both hands, and stir.

Beside me, Jennifer leans against the counter and talks about her trip to visit her friend Kim at USC. I nod absently as I stir, interrupting once. "Can you grab a couple plates?" I ask.

Jennifer turns to open the cupboard, selects two dinner plates, and lays them on the counter.

I look at the spoon gripped in my left hand and wonder how it got there. I eye the pan on the stove. Pasta, I think, and fumble as I switch hands with the spoon. I grip the handle of the pan with my left hand and eye the distance between pan and plate. With my right hand I scoop a spoonful of pasta, then aim for the closest plate, but the food falls off my spoon before it reaches the plate. I frown, release the pan and, with both hands, attempt to scoop the pasta off the kitchen counter and onto the plate.

Suddenly, Jennifer's hands shoot out to grab mine. "Stop it," she orders. "You're scaring me." I look at my daughter's smooth, young hands grasping mine. I feel warmth and strength seeping through my skin, hear concern and worry in her voice.

I look blankly into Jennifer's warm brown eyes, liquid chocolate like Jack's, and remember a time long ago when she was seven. Jack was out of town that day, in the midst of his usual weekly commute to Sacramento, so I had raced home after work, arriving just in time to greet the neighbor who carpooled Jennifer home from school. My heart pounded in my head then, too, though that time with worry: worry that I couldn't navigate Santa Barbara traffic with enough skill and speed, worry that my neighbor would think less of me as a mother for not being there when my daughter returned home from school, worry that Jen would be left home alone, worry that she would worry. But Jennifer had smiled, wrapped her arms around me, and talked about a classmate's birthday party at school that day.

"When does Stripes get a birthday?" Jennifer had asked, bending to greet her cat. "Cats should have birthdays too."

I smiled. "Let's say next week."

"Do you hear that, Stripes?" Jennifer hugged her cat. "You're one year old. We're going to have a birthday party for you."

~~~

The grip on my hands tightens. "Mom," Jennifer repeats, "you're scaring me. Something's not right."

As if from a great distance I see myself standing in the kitchen with my daughter, no longer a child of seven who planned the birthday party of a beloved pet. I see steam rising from the hot pan on the stove and the splash of red sauce along the kitchen counter, see my daughter's smooth hands shake mine, as if to shake some sense into me, to shake me back to the world she knew where mothers are capable, able to put food on a dish for their daughters and serve it at the table.

"You're right," I say. "I must be sick."

"You go to bed. I'll clean up."

"Maybe I should lie down."

"Do you have work tomorrow?"

"Is tomorrow Tuesday?" I ask.

"Promise me you'll call the doctor first. I'll drive you. Doctor before work. Promise, Mom."

I sigh. Who's the parent, and who's the child now? But she's right. Headaches shouldn't last this long. I nod and turn to shamble out of the kitchen. "I'll call in the morning. Right now, I'm going to bed."

CHAPTER SIX

French Hospital Emergency Room
Dawn, Tuesday, April 4, 2006

I doze fitfully. As before, I watch the clock pass ten o'clock, eleven o'clock, twelve, yet time is a blur and means nothing. Jennifer appears throughout the night, tiptoeing into the darkened room to stand at my bed, listening to me breathe. "I'm okay, honey," I say once when I open my eyes to see her figure, backlit by the hall light, standing beside me.

~~~

A noise rouses me, a new sound that doesn't belong in the semi-awake darkness of my night. Holding my head as still as possible, I turn my eyes toward the bedside clock, my companion throughout the night. Four a.m. I hear the bedroom door click closed, the handle turning with a whispered sigh. Soft footsteps pad the length of the hall. In the distance, another door gently closes, a bed creaks, and then all is silent.

Slowly I shift my gaze toward my bedroom door. The shaft of moonlight shining through my bedroom window highlights the stack of papers strategically placed so I will see it the minute I get up in the morning. Has she been awake this whole time? I stare until curiosity forces me to gingerly lift my head from the pillows. I swing my legs over the side of the bed, pause to let the pounding in my head settle into an easier rhythm, and go to see.

Jennifer's childlike scrawl fills the top sheet. "Dear Mom, I am very worried about you. I think you are having a stroke. Please don't go to work this morning until you see a doctor."

My hands shake as I muddle through the pages Jen has printed from the internet. My daughter has logged on to medical websites and followed links until she discovered what she was looking for: information about early warning signs for strokes and stroke symptoms. Realization hits me like a fist to my gut. With sudden clarity, I see the previous ten days: misplaced keys, the fall up a curb, my hands struggling on the computer keyboard, a shattered glass in the kitchen, dropped swim gear, a messy checkbook.

She's right, I think. Something is wrong. I need to go to the emergency room.

I flop the bedcovers back, then stop. First, a shower. Can't shower in the hospital. Hot water sounds good. I stand under the hot shower, head bowed, hand on cool tiles to steady myself, not listening to the beat in my head, not thinking of my daughter worrying at the computer into the early morning hours, not letting my mind go beyond anything other than how good the hot water feels. I slowly towel myself off with flaccid hands, struggle into jeans and T-shirt left on my bedroom floor the night before, and shove my feet into a nearby pair of clogs. I blast my hair into an unruly mop, struggling to hold the hair dryer in my left hand, and turn to look at the clock: 4:45. I hesitate in the hallway, noting Jennifer's closed bedroom door. She's been awake all night. I can't wake her up now.

I grasp the staircase railing with both hands and sidestep downstairs to where Missy waits in the semi-darkness. The dog pants softly, her ears perked in anticipation of an earlier-than-usual morning walk. "No, Miss," I mutter. "Backyard." The golden retriever, happy with the unexpected companionship, circles the backyard grass. I wait and watch serrated stars fade from the night sky. The dawn is cold, the ground wet with rain. Against the encroaching light, Islay Hill emerges, not as the gently rounded hill it is, but rather as a sharp-toothed, jagged outline above the backyard fence. I'm going to the hospital, I think. Something's wrong. Maybe it's my eyes. I try the word out again. *Hospital.*

In the garage I struggle to start my car, attempting three times to put the key in the ignition until I finally steady it with both hands. I draw the seatbelt across my chest, but my right hand is numb, and I can't feel where the seatbelt should fit. It's only two miles, I think, and leave the seatbelt draped across my chest as I drive, my left hand steering the car down dark residential streets to French Hospital.

Garish emergency room lights slash the early morning dimness. I park my car in an empty space under a streetlight. I don't know when I'll return, and I want the car to be visible in the darkened hospital parking lot. I take a seat in an orange vinyl chair in the emergency waiting room. Through an opaque privacy screen propped between waiting room and nurse's station I see a figure sitting at a desk.

"Be right with you," a voice calls.

I close my eyes, breathe deeply, and massage my head with hands that shake.

"Okay," the voice calls. "Come on back."

I round the screen, my legs buckling beneath me as I lower myself into a chair.

"What seems to be the problem?" the nurse asks.

"Headache," I mutter as I massage my temples.

"Headache?" the nurse asks.

"Migraine," I answer, pointing to my head, and burst into tears.

CHAPTER SEVEN

Dawn Patrol

I have never had a migraine, don't really know what one feels like, but because my headache is so severe, I don't know what else to call it. The emergency room nurse pushes a tissue box across the desk and, in a conversation punctuated by my tears, begins her questioning.

"Where does it hurt?"

I rub a hand across my forehead to the temples. "Here. And here." I rub the top and sides of my head.

"How long have you had a headache?"

I wipe my eyes before answering. "A couple weeks."

"Has the pain been this bad for the entire two weeks?"

I shake my head, wince, then rub my hand again across my forehead. "No. Few days."

"Do you get migraines often?"

"I've never had one."

"Never had one?"

"Never."

"Why do you think it's a migraine?"

"It's the only thing I can think to call it."

She finishes entering data into the computer, copies the insurance card I dig out of my wallet, and stands. "Let's get you settled in a bed, get the doctor in to see you. He may want to run some tests." She has my elbow now as she buzzes me through the door leading from her desk area into the emergency room and stops next to an empty bed. "This gown opens in the back. You can leave your shoes and clothes on this chair. I have some paperwork I'll bring back for you to sign, and then we'll see what's going on in that head of yours."

I struggle out of my jeans, then tussle with the hospital gown, finally giving up on tying it in the back with a right hand that is progressively useless. I sink into bed, my head against a stack of pillows. I heave a sigh, wanting to be anywhere but in a hospital. I close my eyes, and as I wait, I imagine the simpler dawns of childhood and drift on the sea of memory.

~~~

"Whose turn is it today?" I asked with all the authority a whispering ten-year-old can muster. Together we huddled, five shapes blurred in the soft dark of early morning. In the predawn shadows, I studied the four tousled heads before me: my soldiers, decked in flannel nightclothes, reporting for duty.

"I'll do it." David, eight years old and two years my junior, was my second in command.

"No. Let me." Dan shot to his feet. His sturdy frame swelled with importance.

"Shush." Leslee, seven, frowned at her younger brother. "You'll wake up Mom and Dad."

"Let me," Dan whispered as he rocked first on one foot and then the next. I could see his white-blond hair, alive in the darkness of the bedroom. "Me," he whispered again and thumped his stout chest with a chubby hand, lest I misunderstand.

I looked over my troops and weighed my decision. David was my usual choice to send on plum assignments. He could steal down the dark hallway and disappear into the shadows. He knew the kitchen well. When his groping hands discovered the old cookie jar, he would silently lift the oft-cracked-and-repaired lid and pillage the treasure: one cookie for each conspirator.

I turned my attention to the third in line. Leslee lacked the requisite bravery. She had once reappeared white-faced and cookie-less, scuttling through the door with a thump and a tale of yellow eyes and the click of toenails on the kitchen floor. Later, when I determined that the monster was nothing more than the old kitchen clock that glowed yellow in the dark and ticked to an uneven rhythm, I relieved her of duty. Toni, four, was too little to reach the counter.

I turned to study my volunteer. Five-year-old Dan was eager for his turn. "All right, Dan, you can go. Just be quiet."

My little brother hunched his shoulders, tilted his head back, and looked me square in the eye. "Okay," he said.

I'm not sure how our game started or even who had created it. Nor have I any remembrance of how long we had done this. It was not an activity borne of necessity because we were five of the best-loved, most-well-fed children in the neighborhood. It was not our intention to thwart our parents' authority or to challenge them in any way. It had more to do with covert operations, of stealthy treks through the sleeping house, and the celebration of a successful mission with co-conspirators. Plain and simple, it was fun.

We remaining four settled back to wait. David stood guard at the bedroom door. Toni leaned against my side; two bright eyes peeked over a podgy hand that pressed against the giggle that threatened to escape. Leslee sat in the center of the bed and draped a quilt over her head, a small lump under an expanse of faded pink cloth.

I tapped her head. "What're you doing in there?"

An impish face framed by a riot of brown curls emerged from under the covers. "I'm a princess," she announced.

"Shhh." David and I spoke as one.

"I'm a princess," she whispered. "I'm locked in a dungeon, and I haven't had any food for a long time. Prince Charming is going to bring me some food."

"Prince Charming? Dan?" I snort.

Leslee was indignant. "No, if I'm a princess, then he's a prince." She retreated to her dungeon under the covers and resumed her story. "I'm a Chinese princess because I'm from China, and I've been kidnapped. And I have long blond hair."

"Humph."

"I have long blond hair." Leslee was adamant. "I need food so I won't starve, so the prince is going to bring me a special cookie with magical powers and save me."

A soft scratch at the bedroom door interrupted the story. David stiffened, then slanted a look at me. The door cracked open, and Dan, his eyes bright with excitement, slipped inside.

"They're good ones today. Oatmeal with white stripes." Dan stood tall, like a brave warrior returning from the hunt, the bounty clutched in one hand, before he crumpled into a fit of giggles.

"Good work," I said. "Don't forget to give one to the princess in the dungeon."

We savored the forbidden treat in silence, five conspirators united for the common good. It had been a successful tour of duty.

I saw him first. The door swung wide, and in the yawning blackness of the open doorway he stood: a darker silhouette framed against the early morning dusk. One hand emerged from the shadows. I watched it fumble against the wall below the light switch, then above it, before finding its mark. I was frozen, helpless to stop his discovery.

We were caught, like deer in the headlights of an eighteen-wheeler. Four cookie-filled hands stopped halfway to four mouths; four sets of eyes riveted on the man in the doorway. He rubbed his eyes once, then again. A hand stroked his jaw as he surveyed the room. He struggled for composure. In that moment of stillness that stretched to the moon and back, I watched his eyes crinkle at the corners and his hand press against a mouth that threatened to smile, and I remembered to breathe.

In the silence, from deep down in her pink cocoon of a dungeon, the princess spoke: "These cookies sure are good."

"What cookies?" my father asked.

I smile at the memory.

CHAPTER EIGHT

A Shadow in My Brain
Early Morning, Tuesday, April 4, 2006

The lights in French Hospital's emergency room are piercing and hurt my eyes. I'm dressed in hospital garb; my mismatched clothes of early morning drape the pink plastic chair at my bedside. I semi-recline against a stack of pillows and rub my temples.

The emergency room doctor I had met earlier approaches me with clipboard and pen in hand. "The CAT scan is inconclusive. We'd like your permission to do a spinal tap."

"No," I say instinctively, never stopping the massage motion of my hands. "No spinal tap."

He crouches next to me. His face is lined with fatigue, and I feel a flash of sympathy for him. "We may not be able to determine the cause of your headache without one." I don't answer, and he continues, "It's time for the changing of the guard. I'm going off duty. I'll share your information with the emergency room doctor coming in. He can talk to you."

I nod. Through the slits of my eyes I watch him cross the room to greet a man decked in scrubs who has just entered the emergency room. At first I think this second doctor is younger, louder, more jovial. No, I correct myself, he's rested. Fresher. Two heads hover over the clipboard, then the first doctor points to the corner of the room where I am, and both heads swivel to study me. I feign sleep. They disappear behind a curtain of mauve and gray drapes.

I reach for my cell phone and try to call Jennifer. No answer on her cell, no answer on the home phone. No surprise. I glance at the time display on the front of my cell phone. Seven thirty. I sigh and know I'll never wake her. I close my eyes, wish I were anywhere other than in the emergency room, alone. I think of my father, gone six years now but never far from my thoughts.

"Mrs. O'Connell?"

My eyes open to find the second emergency room doctor standing at the foot of my bed, his eyes behind wire-frame glasses appraising, his demeanor somber. "Mrs. O'Connell, we've had a clearer look at your CAT scan. We see a shadow that we think is a mass."

"Mass?"

"Tumor."

"Tumor."

"Tumor."

"In my head?"

"In your brain."

"In my brain?" I'm a parrot, repeating words that have no meaning to me.

"In your brain. We'd like to evaluate you further for a possible brain tumor."

"Okay," I say. "How do we do that?"

"You're going to Sierra Vista," he says, referring to the hospital across town. "They have access to better MRI equipment than we have here."

"Okay," I say, thinking that I'll drive myself. "When?"

"A few minutes. We'll call the ambulance now."

Ambulance. I digest that word while I pick up my cell phone and call Jennifer.

Both phones, no answer. I try her again. And again.

At eight o'clock I call Jack's cell phone. I know he is in Sacramento, but I need to talk, and he needs to know.

"H'lo?"

"Jack?"

"Hey. That's funny. I just turned my cell phone on."

"Where are you?"

"Work. I had an early meeting, and we just finished, and I'm on my way to a speech, so I came into the office to turn my phone on. A minute earlier you wouldn't have reached me, and a minute later I'd have been gone. What's up?"

"I'm at the hospital."

"Hospital?"

"Hospital. French Hospital. They think I have a brain tumor."

"What?"

"A brain tumor."

"A brain tumor?"

"A brain tumor."

He is silent, as stunned as I am. "You've got to be kidding."

"Nope."

"Man." Then, "I should come."

"I wish you would."

"Man. I've been patting myself on the back, feeling so smart for getting up here before the storm hit."

"Storm?"

"A major storm in northern California. Airports are closed, planes are grounded."

"How will you get here?"

"I don't know. I'll think of something. Are you there by yourself?"

"Yeah."

"Where's Jen?"

"She was up late researching my symptoms on the internet. She's only been asleep a couple hours. I didn't have the heart to wake her when I left. Can you reach her?"

"Yeah, I'll call her. You're at French?"

"I'm being moved to Sierra Vista. Come to Sierra Vista."

"Okay. Sierra Vista. I don't know how or when I'll get there, but I'll be there."

"I'll wait here." My weak attempt at a joke falls flat.

"Brain tumor?"

"Brain tumor."

"Hang in there. I'll get there as soon as I can."

CHAPTER NINE

Sierra Vista Hospital
Midmorning, Tuesday, April 4, 2006

My first ambulance ride is unremarkable. No lights, no sirens, no roaring through shortcuts in a mad dash to save the patient strapped inside. We reach Sierra Vista Hospital in ten minutes. I'm lifted from the ambulance on the gurney, rolled through double glass doors, and admitted to my second hospital for the day. I am housed temporarily in the emergency room until an MRI can be arranged. I do the best I can with the intake paperwork. A nurse holds the documents steady as I switch the pen to my left hand to sign my name. She retrieves the pen from where it's slipped below the bedcovers and leaves. I close my eyes to block out harsh lights and disjointed thoughts and doze.

I'm roused from my semi-awake state when the bed begins to move. An ambulance attendant pulls at the foot railings; another is at my side, IV bag held high. Funny, I don't remember the IV, yet it's clearly inserted into my arm. From behind me, the third attendant speaks.

"Good morning, Mrs. O'Connell. We've got a short drive to San Luis MRI. We'll get you taken care of and get you back here. Is there anybody here we should talk to, let them know where you'll be?"

"No," I answer, feeling suddenly alone. "They haven't caught up with me yet."

"Well, then, we'll have you back before they even know you're gone."

I'm lifted again into the back of an ambulance but barely settle into the rhythm of the ride before we stop again.

"We're there?" I ask.

"We're there."

"Short ride."

"I can't quite get you to the door," the attendant says, and I feel the rain soft against my face. "We have to roll you the rest of the way. I'll try to shield you."

"No," I say. "It feels good."

The MRI passes in a blur. Afterwards, I relish the rain across my face as I'm wheeled out to the waiting ambulance. Back at Sierra Vista I'm taken to the CCU, the Critical Care Unit.

"Can I get you anything?" a nurse asks.

"Water, please," I answer.

She pours a glass and sets the pink plastic pitcher next to it. I eye the glass of water and wonder how to drink it.

"How about a straw?"

I nod. "I need one."

"We have a call in to Dr. Segal. He's the on-call neurologist. He'll be in to see you shortly."

Dr. Segal. It's a name I know. I've been in his office before. Not as a patient, but years ago as a court reporter when I took his deposition in a court case. When he arrives, I don't like what he has to say.

"Brain tumor," he says. "Inoperable."

"Brain tumor?" I ask.

"Brain tumor."

"Inoperable?"

"Inoperable."

"What does that mean?"

"It means we can't operate."

He says more, but I stop listening.

Hours pass in a hushed blur. I'm aware of nurses moving in and out of my partitioned section of the CCU. My blood pressure and temperature are taken, and I respond to questions posed. I can hear Dr. Segal's voice on the other side of the curtain and pick out words: Jack O'Connell . . .

senator... flying... weather... Jack O'Connell. I know he's made the connection between me and Jack, an association that normally annoys me—not because I'm not proud of my husband's public and personal accomplishments, but because I don't like impressing others with the simple fact of his career. Today, however, I'm grateful. Dr. Segal is awaiting Jack's arrival as eagerly as I am.

It's nearly three o'clock when I sense the change in energy outside my curtained cocoon. Voices are louder, more animated. A conversation starts, stops. I'm weak with relief when I hear Jack's voice.

The curtain parts, and Jack pops his head in. His face is etched with fatigue and worry. "Hey, you," he says. "What's up?"

"It's inoperable," I blurt out.

"What?"

"Inoperable."

"Man."

"Yeah."

"Who told you that?"

"Dr. Segal. I don't think I like him very much. He told me it was inoperable and left it at that. Ask Don and Ray what they know about him," I said, referring to our two trial lawyer friends. San Luis Obispo is a small town; lawyers have opinions about doctors and vice versa. "Find out what they know."

"He told you it's inoperable?"

"He said more, but that's all I heard. He wanted to wait for you."

The curtain behind Jack opens, and Dr. Segal enters the room. His smile is genial as he slaps Jack on the back. "It's nice to meet you," he says. "Glad you're here. We have a decision to make."

"Did you tell my wife her brain tumor is inoperable?" Jack asks.

"Yes. It is."

"It is?"

"Yes. Here."

"Here?"

"Here. At Sierra Vista. We can't handle a surgery like this. You're looking at one of the big teaching hospitals: UCLA, Stanford, or UCSF."

"She'll be able to have surgery at one of those?"

"It's her only chance."

"Which one do you recommend?"

"Any of those facilities will be able to handle a neurosurgery of the brain."

Jack is pensive for a moment, then asks, "Let me put it this way: If this were your wife, where would you take her?"

Dr. Segal pauses to think. "You know," he begins slowly, "there is a brilliant neurosurgeon in San Francisco. I heard him present at a conference. Very impressive. His name is Dr. Berger, Mitchel Berger. He teaches and practices at UCSF and is on the cutting edge of all the new technology in brain surgery. He'd be my first choice."

"Then we're asking for him," Jack said.

"You want Dr. Berger?"

"We want Dr. Berger. How do we contact him?"

"I'll call him, see if we can get you in."

"We'll wait here," Jack says and turns to me. "All right?"

"All right."

When Dr. Segal is gone, I sigh with relief. "Thank god you're here."

"I almost didn't make it."

"Is it still raining outside?"

Jack snorts. "Raining? Try a hundred-year storm. Planes are grounded in both Sacramento and San Francisco."

"How'd you get here?"

"We called the CHP, but their plane was grounded in Santa Rosa, so a patrolman offered to drive me. We started out by car, had the flashers and lights on and everything, and made it about thirty miles south of Sacramento before we received the call to turn around to meet the CHP plane at Executive Field in Sacramento. Apparently, two CHP pilots volunteered to try to get me to San Luis Obispo. They flew from Santa Rosa, picked me up in Sacramento, and brought me home."

"Wow."

"Wow is right. I think we went sideways across the sky more often than straight ahead."

"You shouldn't have tried that."

"I wouldn't have if they weren't so confident." Jack shakes his head. "In retrospect, it might have been easier to drive. What's normally an hour-long flight turned into a very rough two-and-a-half hours."

"Oh, no, Jack. Don't tell me that."

"I know. There was one point where I thought, 'I'm not going to be any good to her if I don't make it.' But the pilots were great, very calm and assured. One of them told me his wife is a superintendent and that I'd recently met her when I toured one of the schools in her district. And I do remember her telling me her husband is a CHP officer."

"We owe them."

"I know. Big time. The pilots told me they were going to stay and have lunch at the Spirit of San Luis," Jack said, referring to the airport restaurant. "I went ahead of them, handed the restaurant owner thirty dollars—you know, the older guy we always talk to—and told him that two CHP pilots were on their way in and lunch was on me."

"That was decent of you. Did Jennifer pick you up?"

"Teri did," Jack says, referring to the wife of our friend Don. "I called Don, Don called Teri. I never could reach Jen on her phone."

"Me neither."

"Frustrating."

"She was up till at least four o'clock," I remind him, "looking up my symptoms on the internet. I didn't have the heart to wake her. I figured I'd be home before she woke up. Denial, I guess. Where is she now?"

"I finally called your mom, and she went over to the house to wake her up. And then I called Don. Teri's been with Jen today too. Teri got me at the airport, took me home, had a turkey sandwich waiting for me when I got there. We had lunch, and then Teri, Jen, your mom, and I came here. Coleen has been sitting outside your room all day," Jack adds, referring to the wife of our friend Ray. "Did you know that?"

I shake my head. "I know nothing. I'm so glad you're here," I say again.

CHAPTER TEN

Ambulance Ride to UCSF
Evening, Tuesday, April 4, 2006

It's nine thirty at night when I'm finally wheeled out of Sierra Vista Hospital's CCU. Friends Coleen and Teri sit vigil in the waiting room most of the day but are never allowed in to see me. Throughout the day I've visited with my mom and brother David. Jack, of course, stays near. It's not until I leave the curtained alcove where I've spent the last twelve hours that I finally see Jennifer. She stands apart from the group clustered around me, her head tilted back to prevent tears from falling. I see them, though, and it's all I can do to blink back my own.

"What's the plan?" I ask.

"Still stormy," Jack answers. "We've been waiting to see if the medevac plane can fly, but it's too risky. You're going by ambulance."

"To San Francisco?"

"To UCSF."

"Okay," I say. "I can do that. Fourth ambulance ride today."

"Jen and I will follow in the morning."

I grab my daughter's hand as I'm wheeled past her. "I'll be okay," I say. "I'll see both of you tomorrow."

She squeezes my hand and nods, unable to speak.

At the door of the emergency room I am shifted to the gurney and rolled to the waiting ambulance. An attendant jumps into the back and guides the gurney along one side of the ambulance where it is fastened to the floor. The gurney is narrow, and I grip the edges, fearful of rolling off during the trip, until the attendant reaches across me and straps me in at several points. "Okay?" he asks. At my nod he taps the window that separates the back from the cab. "We're good to go," he tells the driver, then straps himself in on a jump seat across from me.

"Two of you?" I ask.

"Two of us. I'm Mike." He points through the window at the back of the cab to the driver and gives me the driver's name. I don't catch it.

"I'm Doree."

He reaches for my wrist and counts the beats of my pulse, then checks the IV bag that's suspended above me before he speaks again. "We'll share the driving, switch halfway. One of us will always be in the back with you. How do you feel?"

"Okay." I close my eyes. "I'll try to sleep." After a moment I add, "Thank you. Long night for you."

"We've been on hold, waiting to see what happens with the weather."

"I heard that. It's been raining all day?"

"Raining hard." He pauses, then asks bluntly, "What's wrong with you?"

I open my eyes to study him. The puzzlement etched on his youthful face is clear. I answer him simply: "Brain tumor."

"Bummer."

"Bummer is right."

"I was just wondering. You don't seem to be in any distress, and you're lucid when you talk. How did you know you had a brain tumor?"

"I didn't. I thought I had a migraine that wouldn't end."

"Why UCSF?"

"Sierra Vista is not equipped to handle a surgery like that, and apparently there is a neurosurgeon at UCSF who specializes in this kind of thing."

"Well, then, you're going to the right place." He settles back against his chair and adjusts the light. "Would you mind if I read?"

"Of course not. Please, go ahead. I'm all right." Being an avid reader, I add, "Got a good book?"

Mike grins. "A murder mystery. I'm almost to the 'whodunit' part."

"Then, by all means, read. Hope it's a surprise ending." And I close my eyes to doze.

What seems but a short while later the ambulance slows, then curves down the off-ramp and stops near a row of lighted buildings. Mike again presses fingers against the pulse in my wrist. His head is turned away, and I can see the lighted dial of the watch on his left wrist he has raised close to his face. He turns back to me and sees me watching him. "You okay?"

I nod. "I'm okay."

"We're taking a break. We're in King City," he says, referring to a small town ninety miles north of San Luis Obispo. "Legally we have to take a short break. We'll grab some food and change places. Can I get you anything?"

"Thank you, no. I'm good."

"Be back," he says, and as he opens the back door of the ambulance to jump down, I see rain illuminated against light posts, streaking against windows and ponding on the asphalt.

"I'll wait here," I say, my weak attempt at humor.

When the ambulance's back doors open again ten minutes later, I see the driver climb aboard. He fastens the door, checks my pulse and the IV bag, straps himself into the jump seat near my head, and taps on the window, all in silence. The light is dimmed. I feel the engine turn over and sense the swaying motion of a rolling vehicle. Halfway, I think, closing my eyes again, but halfway to what I don't know.

~~~

It's after one o'clock in the morning when the ambulance slows, pulls left into a hard circle, then backs into the emergency entrance to the University of California, San Francisco Medical Center. I've arrived, yet I know my journey is just beginning. Events have happened too fast for fear to sink in. I feel numb, but mostly I alternate between disbelief and hope. Intellectually, I know that UCSF is an academic institution, one of ten campuses in the University of California system. I know, too, that because it is a teaching hospital, being here offers me greater options than either of the two community hospitals I've been in today. I think of innovative, cutting-edge medical knowledge and state-of-the-art technology and know that if I can be helped, it will happen here.

What I don't know yet but will soon discover is that UCSF is among the top five hospitals in the nation in the fields of neurosurgery and neurology, and it is home to one of the largest brain tumor centers in the United States as well. All this and more I'll learn in the coming days. For now, I am simply here.

~~~

The corridors are bright, the walls a clean, institutional beige, the elevator slow but large enough to accommodate a gurney and two attendants. I see myself as if from a great distance, watch as that woman is wheeled down a long hallway, the pallor in her face caused by a combination of harsh fluorescent lights and worry. Mike keeps up a running commentary; I'm not sure if I answer. The elevator doors open, and I'm deposited on the eleventh floor.

"Well, Mrs. O'Connell, here you are," says a voice much too cheery for the wee hours of the morning. "We've been waiting for you."

I smile and answer the nurse in kind. "Thanks for waiting. I got here as fast as I could."

Mike reaches across me and hands my chart to the charge nurse, and I feel the gurney begin to roll again. "We've been saving a room for you," the nurse says. "Didn't know when you'd finally get here. We'll get you into bed, let you rest up tonight before the doctor comes to see you in the morning."

I'm wheeled into a large, dimly lit hospital room, and when I'm finally unstrapped from the gurney, I sit up. I've spent most of the day on my back, and with that sudden movement I sway slightly and grimace at the throbbing in my head. The pounding is so loud I'm surprised the others don't hear it. The nurse grabs my arm. "Wait for us. We need to transfer you to the bed."

"She can probably do it herself," Mike says.

I nod. "I can do it," I say, and as I swing my feet over the side of the gurney, I feel three pairs of hands steadying me.

When I'm settled in bed with the IV bag hung above me and the call button tucked in at my side, I turn to the two ambulance attendants. "Thank you," I say. "Terrific driving through all that rain."

"You're welcome." Mike pats my bed. "You take care," he says before they turn to gather their equipment and retrace their steps back to the waiting ambulance. His friendly presence and lighthearted chatter throughout the night have helped ease my fears. I haven't even thought the words *brain tumor* at all in the last several hours; my mind hasn't allowed me to face the gravity of my illness or how drastically my life has changed in one short day.

I'm still now, no longer on the move. The room is dark and peaceful. I sense worry and fear nibbling at the edges of my consciousness. I acknowledge them but don't let them in. Not yet. I'm in the hospital, at UCSF Medical Center. I'm where I need to be to begin to sort through what has happened, to get my mind in a place where I can handle what's still to come. And I have a doctor to see tomorrow. I have to make sense—no hysteria allowed.

Mike pops his head back through the door. "Good luck," he says. I'm sorry to see him go.

CHAPTER ELEVEN

UCSF and Dr. Berger
Early, Wednesday, April 5, 2006

Thirty years ago, when I was a college student, an English instructor posed the following question to our class: If you were neck deep in horse shit (his word), would you want to be told that you were, in fact, neck deep in horse shit, or would you rather be told that you were neck deep in rose petals? A lively discussion followed until our teacher put the issue to a vote. To my surprise, I was one of three people who voted to be told the truth.

I think of that now—now that I'm in a hospital bed waiting to hear my future.

Do I still want the truth, or would I be happier with sugarcoating? Last night, I deliberately practiced the business of rest: peaceful breathing and images of rushing water. In my mind, I listened to rocks tumble, felt sun across my back. But then, even in my visualization, a hawk shrieked, water splashed my face, anxiety loomed.

In the early morning darkness, fitful thoughts fill my head. Is it still raining? Are Jack and Jen on the road? Who's watching the dog? Has someone called my work? What will happen to me? Surgery, or ... but when I get close to the reason why I'm in the hospital, my thoughts veer in another direction. Reality is frightening, and I am unable to face facts. I have always prided myself on facing troubles head on, and it's all I can do to keep from unhooking the IV and walking out.

I'm saved from myself by the arrival of Dr. Berger. The subtle gray of dawn has arrived, unnoticed until I hear the tap at the door. A head pokes around the corner, followed by a white doctor's coat. Mitchel S. Berger, Harvard-educated professor of neurosurgery and chair of the Neurological Surgery Department at UCSF, is a nationally recognized expert in treating brain and spinal cord tumors in adults and children. He is co-director of the Adult Brain Tumor Surgery Program and director of the Brain Tumor Research Center; he also sits on the American Board of Neurological Surgeons. More importantly, at least for me, he's a specialist in brain mapping techniques used to identify areas of motor, sensory, and language function during surgery and an expert in the use of the gamma knife for tumor treatment.

These things and more I learn later, but for now, I content myself with his appearance: tall, mid-fifties, tanned face beneath a shock of white hair, and steady hands. He enters the hospital room. I feel an aura of strength and confidence, of intelligence, of gentleness. His brown eyes never waver from mine as he pulls a chair near my bed and takes my hand.

Mrs. O'Connell," he says. "You're here."

"I'm here."

"We expected you last night, but I understand the roads were treacherous, and the skies even more so. You arrived about one o'clock, one thirty?"

"1:20." When he raises his eyebrows, I add, "I noticed the clock as I was wheeled in."

"Good," he says. "Are you here alone?"

"My husband and daughter are on their way."

"Good," he says again. "I've had a chance to see your scans. Has anyone told you why you're here?"

"I have a brain tumor." Funny. I can say the words now in his calm presence.

"You do. And we're going to take care of it."

"Today?"

"Tomorrow. Tests today, surgery tomorrow."

"Okay."

Dr. Berger releases my hand and sits back in his chair. "Tell me a little bit about yourself."

"What would you like to know?"

"Who you are, if you work, what you like to do in your free time. Things like that."

"Okay. Well, I'm fifty. Been married twenty-nine years and have a nineteen-year-old daughter. I work at Cal Poly."

"What do you do at Cal Poly?"

"I work in the Construction Management Department. That's in the College of Architecture and Environmental Design."

"What do you do there?"

"Clerical work. Whatever the professors in that department need. I'm a temporary hire, too, though they just asked me to stay on."

"Temporary?"

"Temporary. I took that position because it was a three-month hire, and I wanted to make some money for a trip to Italy."

"Italy, huh? You like to travel?"

"I want to travel. I haven't done much."

"What did you do before this job?"

"Took classes, writing classes. Worked in my husband's office. Volunteered at the Literacy Council. I was a court reporter for nearly twenty years. Substitute taught very briefly."

"Are you a teacher?"

"I hold a credential but am not teaching now."

"Do you want to teach?"

"No. I really don't. I discovered halfway through the credential program that I'd rather work with adults. I have great respect for English language learners and enjoyed the Literacy Council, and I like being at Cal Poly."

"How physically active are you?"

"Not as much as I should be. Before I began at Cal Poly, I walked twice a week with a friend, anywhere from four to six miles, depending on the trail we'd take. And I swam twice a week with my husband on weekends. Just the swimming since I've been back at work."

Dr. Berger, his eyes now pointed towards the ceiling, nods his head. He's quiet for a moment, in thought.

"Where's my tumor?" I blurt out.

"That's just what I'm thinking about," Dr. Berger answers. "Left parietal lobe. Right about here," and he touches the left side of my head above my ear. "What were your symptoms? How did you know to go to the hospital?"

"I thought I was having about a week's worth of migraines."

"Do you get migraines?"

"I've never had one. I just thought what I was experiencing must be a migraine."

"Anything else?"

"Stumbling. Making mistakes at work. I couldn't remember a short series of numbers to enter into the computer. I couldn't even figure out where to put my hands on the keyboard. A hard time grasping words and ideas. A hard time picking things up with my hands. I blamed everything on headaches and being fifty. I still would have been denying that I was sick if my daughter hadn't insisted I see a doctor."

"Good for her. How about now? Are you having any neurological difficulties with the right side of your body?"

I raise my right hand. "I can't hold a pen in my right hand. And that happened fast."

"The left side of the brain controls the right side of the body, and vice versa. An injury to the left hemisphere of the brain will be noticed on the right, like your hand. The left brain is the linear, analytical side. It deals more with language and helps to analyze information and puts things in order. The right hemisphere is more related to visual activities and creative thought. That's simplified, but it gives you an idea of the specific roles each side of our brain plays. Yours is in a difficult location, though, and that's what I'm thinking about right now." Dr. Berger puts his arms straight out in front of him, his palms side by side and parallel to the floor. "Hold your arms out like this."

I do as he directs.

"Okay. Now keep them there and close your eyes."

I do that as well and visualize my arms out straight.

"Stay in that position," Dr. Berger instructs, "and open your eyes."

I gasp. My left arm remains straight and parallel to the ground. My right arm, though, has drifted upward until it's ear-level, and the palm of my hand has turned sideways so that the palm is now perpendicular to the floor. "But I was concentrating," I say. "I couldn't feel that happening."

"That's called pronator drift. Damage to the left parietal lobe can also result in right–left confusion, difficulty with writing, difficulty with mathematics, even with language." He smiles. "I don't see the difficulty with language, but then I don't know you well. Are you having word choice issues? In other words, are you having trouble coming up with the right word to use?"

"Not other than being fifty," I say.

He laughs, then quickly sobers. "Here's the worrisome part. A section of your tumor is right underneath the motor strip. That's the area in the brain that controls movement, all muscle movement in the body, including those muscles used for speech. And that's why we need more tests. I need to know exactly how much space is between the tumor and the motor strip."

Suddenly and finally I let it all in: the falls, the dropped glass, my inability to hold a spoon or a pen or to process numbers, the throbbing, relentless headache, the long ambulance ride, all the anxiety and fears I've held at arm's length. Tears roll down my face. And as I cry, Dr. Berger reaches out to rub my arm.

"I know," he says soothingly. "I know."

I reach for the proffered tissue. "Thanks," I manage. Then, "Sorry."

"No need to apologize. I know how frightening this must be to you."

I take a deep breath, and another, and all the time I am aware of Dr. Berger stroking my arm, calming me.

"Here's what I need to know," he says. "By the end of today we'll know more, but for now, I need to hear from you whether your physical ability is more important to you than your language abilities."

"I have to choose?"

"Just in the event I need to make that decision in surgery." He continues to stroke my arm. "If the tumor can be excised cleanly, this won't be a factor. It's just a good thing to talk about this now."

My answer is easy. "My language. I love to read and write. I belong to a writers group. I enjoy taking classes." I begin to tear up again but catch myself. "Language," I say.

"Good," Dr. Berger says. "Now, I'd like to call your husband, let him know that we've met and that we've talked, let him know a little bit about our schedule for today. May I call him?"

"Of course," I say.

"Do you have his cell phone number?"

"Yes." I rattle off the numbers.

"I'll call him. I'll get the tests scheduled for this morning, and someone will be in to get you. We'll have some answers this afternoon."

"Thank you."

He smiles, gives my arm one more pat, and turns to leave. I lay my head against the mound of pillows at my neck, and by the time the door shuts behind him, I'm asleep.

CHAPTER TWELVE

A Day of Tests
Wednesday, April 5, 2006

My sleep is deep but short-lived. I sense the bustle of the two orderlies before I open my eyes. I feel one tuck the sheet under the thin hospital bed mattress; I watch another disentangle the IV bag from the pole behind my head and attach it to the bed frame. He sees me watching him and answers my unasked question. "You've got a busy schedule today. We're taking you to the imaging center."

"How busy?" I ask.

"All day. Some things you'll be able to sleep through, like the MRI. Some of the tests you'll be answering questions, so the technicians will prompt you to stay awake."

"Okay."

"It's a long day," he adds, "but an important one for the doctor. The more he knows before surgery, the better it is for both of you."

I close my eyes against harsh fluorescent lights that line the long hallway, hear the ping of the elevator door as it opens and again as it closes, sense the drop as the elevator moves downward through the floors. When the doors open again, I'm wheeled into a large, bright room and greeted by technicians in multicolored scrubs.

I soon will learn that magnetic resonance imaging, or MRI, uses magnetic fields and computers to record images of the brain on film.

The standard technique to diagnose suspected brain tumors, an MRI detects signals emitted from abnormal as well as normal tissue. Pictures are taken from different planes in the brain, which permits doctors to create a clear, three-dimensional image of the tumor. Here is where I'll start my tests.

I am directed to lie down on a table and given earplugs. I close my eyes as I am slid through the narrow opening of a long cylindrical tube. A blanket covers me. I know the MRI will consist of loud banging noises caused by the electronics in the machine, so I am not surprised to feel additional padding being placed between my ears and the MRI tube. I remind myself that I am not claustrophobic.

Every hour I'm given a break. The table is rolled out from the metal tube, and I am helped into a sitting position. It's during these short breaks that I glean my best information.

"Why do I have an IV?"

"That's for the contrast."

"What does that mean?"

"It's a dye called gadolinium. We inject it into your vein and it flows into the brain tissue."

"What's the purpose of that?"

"Abnormal or diseased brain tissue absorbs more dye than healthy brain tissue. It highlights any differences and allows the doctor to see a tumor more clearly."

The second time I emerge from the MRI tube for a break I have new questions. "What's the difference between an MRI and a CAT scan?"

"CT scan, or CAT scan, stands for computed tomography. It combines sophisticated computer and X-ray technology and has the ability to show a combination of soft tissue, blood vessels, and bone."

"Why will I have a CAT scan in addition to the MRI?"

"A CT scan can detect swelling, bleeding, or hemorrhage and can determine some types of tumors." The technician pauses, then adds, "What we are trying to determine is if your brain tumor is a primary cancer or if it has metastasized from another organ in your body."

Another organ? I hadn't considered this possibility. Cancer? The word "tumor" has peppered the conversations swirling around me. In fact, I had used that word myself in a casual and matter-of-fact manner. But despite my journey of the past two days, this is the first time I've even thought of cancer. The CAT scan makes a slight clicking noise as it moves. The information gathered is sent to a computer, which translates it into pictures. I'm silent through the scan, alone with my thoughts.

At the conclusion of the CAT scan, I'm allowed to stand, and with a technician's hand under my elbow, I tow the IV pole to the restroom.

Stretched out once again on the narrow MRI table, I'm introduced to the next test. "It's called a functional MRI," the technician says. "It tracks the use of oxygen in your brain, which will give us instant pictures of your brain activity." She lays a blanket over my legs and hands me earplugs before continuing. "Each person's brain is unique, so it also helps to identify the motor, language, and sensory centers of your brain."

"Okay," I say.

"This will be key to planning your surgery. We can see which part of your brain is handling speech, thought, movement, or sensation." She pauses to replace the soft padding at my ears before she rolls me back into the cylindrical tube. I hear an echo as she begins to speak through a microphone in my headset. "Keep your eyes open this time. I have words to show you. They'll flash onto the small window that's at eye level. Can you see it?"

"I see it."

"These are nouns. I'd like you to read the word, then give me a verb that relates to that noun. An action word. For example, if I say *ball*, you might say *roll*, or *bounce*. Got it?"

"Got it."

"Okay. Here's your first word."

I see the card in the mirrored display immediately in front of my eyes. "*Car*," I read, then add, "*green* ." I pause to think. "No, not *green. Driving.*"

She chuckles. "It tests your brain. First you have to know what a noun is, and then you have to know what a verb is. Ready for the next one?"

"I'm ready. *Dog*," I read. "*Walk. Tree. Tall*—I mean *grow.*" It's almost a fun game, and by the time I'm once again rolled out from the

MRI tube, I'm tired from concentrating, but I feel like I've successfully passed the test.

It's two o'clock by the time I'm moved from the imaging room back into my hospital room. Tired of lying on my back, I elect to sit upright in bed as I roll down the hallway. That's fortunate, because I spy Jack and Jennifer checking in at the nurses' station. I wave, the jovial hostess, happy to see her guests. "Hi, guys," I say. "Yay, you're here." I point down the hall in the general direction of my room. "Follow me."

"I see our car," Jack says later. He's standing at the window of my eleventh-floor hospital room, pointing. "See it, Jen?"

She crowds near and peers down. "Oh, yeah. That was a long walk."

"Wet and muddy too." He points. "That's Kezar Stadium."

"Kezar?" I ask. "Isn't that at the edge of Golden Gate Park?"

"Must be. All I know is this is where the 49ers used to play," Jack says, referring to the San Francisco NFL team. "Oakland Raiders at one time too, I think."

"Keep in mind it was pitch black when I got here last night. I have no idea where I am."

Jack turns and grins. "San Francisco. Kezar Stadium."

"And in a hospital," I add.

Jack sobers. "And in a hospital. Did you sleep?"

"Dozed. You?"

Jack shakes his head. "Not much."

"No one did," Jennifer says. "Dad ended up on the couch."

"I think we were just waiting for morning, hoping the rain would let up enough so we could drive."

"Did it?" I ask.

"Better," Jack says.

"Slow," Jennifer adds. "And Dr. Berger called Dad."

Jack nods. "It was about seven o'clock this morning. We were passing through King City. He told us he'd already met with you and that you were doing great and that he'd know more about the surgery after all your tests. What a great guy. He sounded really positive."

"Yeah, that was after he saw me this morning. He asked if he could call you, and I gave him your cell number."

"I think we made the right decision," Jack says.

He talks on, about Kezar Stadium, about Dr. Berger, about the slow and careful drive through monsoon-like rain, about finding the last available street parking in a city notorious for no parking spaces. Jennifer nods and adds her comments. No one seems to want a deeper conversation about brain surgery, or possibilities of survival, or the future. I don't tell Jack about my earlier conversation with Dr. Berger where, worst-case scenario, I elect to preserve my language ability over motor skills. We are talking on the surface, afraid of what we'll discover if we delve deeper. I entertain them with funny descriptions of test questions I missed, of using *green* for an action word, with what an MRI sounds like. I see exhaustion in their faces, an exhaustion that mirrors mine. I see it in the droop of their shoulders, hear it in voices struggling to stay upbeat.

"Where are you staying?" I ask.

"Daly City," Jack says. "I forget the name of the hotel."

"How far is that from here?"

"A half hour, depending on traffic."

"Are you checked in?"

Jack shakes his head.

"We thought we'd find you first," Jen says, "because we didn't know where we were going."

"Have you eaten?" I ask.

"No." Jen shakes her head. "But you know Dad. We were looking for you and he found the cafeteria. It's a big one. Something for everyone."

"You should go. Thank you for being here, but you should go. Have something to eat and find your hotel and get some sleep. I'll see you tomorrow."

I give my husband and daughter each a hug and send them on their way before I lay my head back and close my eyes. I am depleted, an empty vessel. Worries hover heavy in the air, but I push them to the shadowed recesses of the room. I'll take them out later, hold them in my hand, examine them. But not right now. The door opens with a soft swish of air. I turn my head.

"I think we made the right decision," Jack says again. "This is where we need to be."

~~~

It's much later when I hear the knock. Night has fallen, something I realize only when Dr. Berger pushes open the door and hallway light slants across the shadowed room. He flips on a soft overhead light, pulls up a chair, and takes my hand. "Awake?" he asks.

"Getting there," I answer.

"Did your family arrive?"

"Yes, they did. This afternoon. They're at the hotel. They'll be here in the morning."

"Has anyone told them which waiting room to use tomorrow?"

"They were going to check on the way out."

Dr. Berger nods. "I'll find them. You had a very productive day. The tests were thorough, and the results were what we had hoped for."

"Surgery tomorrow morning?"

"Surgery tomorrow morning. You have room between the tumor and the motor strip. A small sliver, but room to maneuver. I think I'll be able to perform the surgery without the need for brain mapping."

"Brain mapping? Like what I did today?"

"Something different. It's an awake craniotomy." At my confused look he explains further. "Brain mapping is a procedure that uses three-dimensional imaging technology during surgery, which allows us to pinpoint the exact parameters of the area to resect. If we needed to do brain mapping, we'd keep you awake for a portion of the surgery. You would talk to us while we stimulate your brain near the tumor site, and we'd be able to identify for certain the functional areas of your brain that control speech, the senses, movement. Once we were able to map out the exact path for surgery, we'd put you back under anesthesia and complete the surgery." He smiles at the look on my face. "Like I said, I don't think we will need to do that." He pats my hand one last time and stands. "Get some sleep. I'll see you in the morning."

"Good night. And thank you," I say.

CHAPTER THIRTEEN

Brain Surgery
Dawn, Thursday, April 6, 2006

Despite my exhaustion, I manage only brief snatches of rest. Worries held at arm's length earlier in the day fill my mind. Tears come; I can no longer push fear away. Later today I'll have brain surgery. My fate and trust are in the hands of Dr. Berger. Throughout the early morning hours nurses pass in and out of my room. One asks if she can pray with me. My temperature is taken, as is my blood pressure. Cool hands lightly pat my arm, hold my wrist, count the beats I hear in my head and feel in my core. Finally, at long last, dawn arrives.

An IV drip is started. I am rolled down the same long hallway under garish fluorescent lights into the elevator. The elevator door pings open, then closed. The drop in my stomach tells me we are descending several floors. Doors slide open and shut again before I'm wheeled into a brightly lit surgical center. Androgynous nurses in scrubs and masks bustle, pushing trays of silver surgical tools, their light blue scrubs shadows against stark white walls. Their eyes and gentle touches tell me that, though this is serious business, they are kind and caring. I am introduced to an anesthesiologist who holds my hand and speaks to me. I don't know what he says. I am sleepy; the drug is working its magic.

Jack and Jennifer tell me later that my surgery took six hours, that Dr. Berger phoned them when it was done, that they met him afterwards at the elevator outside the second-floor surgery center to talk.

I know none of this, of course. It's several hours before I stir in the recovery room. The left side of my head has been shaved. I finger a horseshoe-shaped row of metal staples. My head was opened, I think, trying to wrap my mind around what happened to me. My head was opened and stapled back together. I tilt my head forward, then twist my neck side to side. My head feels full and heavy, but there is no pain. Legs shift on the bed. I feel the squeeze of the circulation pump wrapped on my lower legs, hear the hiss as the pressure is released, feel the pump again. I flex my toes. My hands pluck at the sheets. A nurse appears in the curtained opening.

"Well hello. Welcome back. How do you feel?"

"Okay."

She checks my wristband. "Can you tell me your name and date of birth?"

"Doree O'Connell, October 30." I'm relieved; the words come easily.

"Do you know where you are?"

"Yes, UCSF."

"And why are you here?"

"I had a brain tumor."

"Good. Any pain?"

"Not that I can tell." My hands fret against the IVs, one at the elbow, another in the back of my hand. Both sites are bruised from bleeding into surrounding tissue; both sites itch where tape affixes needles to my skin. "Can I sit up?"

"Not yet. We need you to stay flat for a while." She takes my blood pressure, counts my pulse, scans a thermometer across my forehead, then disappears and returns armed with a cup of water and a pill that she pours from a smaller cup into my hand. I am obedient and swallow the pill. It's not until I request a bucket that I think to ask what it was.

"Vicodin," the nurse says.

"Not good," I say as I empty the contents of my stomach into the basin.

"No more Vicodin," she agrees, and she takes the basin from the room. She returns with a wet washcloth and glass of water. I wipe my face and swish water in my mouth. She cautions me not to swallow.

"Can I sit up?"

"Not yet."

"Can we take this catheter out?"

"Not yet."

My legs shift on the bed. I again note the squeeze of the circulation pump wrapped around my calves, hear again the hiss as the pressure is released, feel the squeeze again. I flex my feet; my hands fret with the sheets. I pluck at the tape affixed to my hand.

The nurse understands. "You were in surgery for a long time," she says. "You received a large dose of drugs through your IVs. Your restlessness comes from the medication leaving your body." She puts her hands on her hips and cocks her head. "Can you take Tylenol with codeine?"

"Not unless you have another bucket."

She smiles. "I don't think I want to give you anything else just yet. Do you have any pain? Headache?"

"None," I say, almost surprised. "None."

"Push the call button if you do. I'll be back to check on you later."

"What floor am I on?"

"What floor?"

"Yes. I know I'm in the recovery room. What floor is this?"

"This is the second floor."

She begins to leave, but I stop her with another question. "What floor is the surgery center?"

"Second floor. Down the hall."

"Second floor, down the hall." I grasp the words and hold on to them as if memorizing my part in a play. Second floor, I think. For some reason it's important to me to know exactly where I am. I'm on the second floor. I was on the eleventh floor before surgery.

The nurse leaves my curtained alcove, and I settle in to think about my journey of the last few days, grateful to be on the recovery side of surgery, grateful to be alive and engaging in conversation, grateful even for the restless fidgeting. Things have happened so fast that I haven't had time to process them. My thoughts are abstract and disjointed. I feel disconnected, as if I am thinking of someone else, that this is something that happened to an acquaintance I once knew in an earlier life and not to me. I wonder why this happened. Not in a "why-did-this-happen-to-me?" sort of way—because really, why not me?—but rather in a deeper, "what-does-this-mean?" sort of way. I don't even form the thought coherently, but I know intuitively this experience will change me and shape the rest of my life.

The recovery room nurse peers around the corner. "Not asleep?"

"No."

"How do you feel?"

"Pretty good."

"Any pain?"

"No."

"Headache?"

"None."

"Well then."

"I can sit up?"

"Let's go part way, see how you feel." She adjusts the bed into a reclining position. "Okay?"

"Okay. Can we take the catheter out?"

She is patient with my impatience. "One step at a time. Let's see how you tolerate this." She stands back and watches me for a moment. "I'll be back. Push the call button if you have any pain or if you feel dizzy."

"I will," I say, and she leaves me with my thoughts.

Much later, I'm in an upright position with the dreaded catheter finally removed when I spy a tall, slim Asian woman through the parted curtains that encircle my bed. Her hair is long, black streaked with gray, and she wears a white lab coat. I watch her sit on an empty bed and scribble furiously in a large medical chart. She closes the chart and reaches into her pocket for a small card. She consults her chart, then jots something on the card. She stands and turns, and our eyes meet. Holding the card in her hand she walks towards me.

"Hi, Mrs. O'Connell. I'm Dr. Susan Chang. I am a neuro-oncologist here at UCSF." She says more, but my mind bumps into the word *oncologist* and can go no further. I've been thinking brain tumor. But cancer? She offers me the card. I take it and speculate why she has scheduled an appointment with me in her office. I nod my head, mumble something unintelligible, and wonder if she senses the hollow feeling in the pit of my stomach. It's just a precaution, I think to myself.

CHAPTER FOURTEEN

Surgery Report and Pathology Report
April 6, 2006

SURGERY REPORT:
April 6, 2006

PREOPERATIVE DIAGNOSIS:
Left parietal glioma

POSTOPERATIVE DIAGNOSIS:
Left parietal glioma

OPERATION:
Left parietal craniotomy, Stealth navigation, microdissection, tumor removal, cortical and subcortical motor mapping.

CLINICAL INDICATIONS:
The clinical history is that of a patient who presents with right upper extremity ataxia and an enhancing mass in the left parietal lobe.

PROCEDURE:
The patient was brought to the operating room and placed in the supine position with the head turned to the right and fixed in the Mayfield

tongs. All extremities were well padded and protected prior to starting, and the scalp fiducials were registered with Stealth navigation. The underlying lesion was drawn on the overlying scalp, and then I proceeded with shaving the head in the usual fashion. After the head was scrubbed, prepped, and draped in the usual fashion, I then made a horseshoe-type incision overlying the lesion and then reflected the scalp and muscle inferiorly. A multiple-hole bone flap just off the midline was turned, and the dura was found to be somewhat tense, although this was alleviated with mannitol and hyperventilation. The dura was then opened, and I could see where the lesion came to the surface and then began to stimulate this whole area, including using strip electrodes under the dura anteriorly, but failed to reveal any evidence of stimulation-induced motor movements up to 16 ma, indicating that the lesion was in the parietal lobe. I then coagulated the cortex overlying this area and the cortex just in front of this, which should have been either the sensory system or the post-sensory gyrus, and then resected down until I found a very necrotic-looking mass, which was resected. I brought in the microscope and continued to resect tumor up to normal margins, and then used subcortical mapping to stimulate the white matter bank anteriorly and inferiorly but failed to reveal any stimulation-induced movement. At this point, I felt I had achieved a gross total resection of this tumor and lined the cavity with Surgicel for perfect hemostasis. The dura was then closed in a watertight fashion, and the bone flap was replaced with plate and screws, followed by closure of the galea with 3 – 0 Vicryl, followed by skin staples. The patient tolerated the procedure well and was taken to the intensive care unit in good condition.

SURGEON:
Berger, Mitchel S., MD

SURGICAL PATHOLOGY:
April 6, 2006

SOURCE:
Brain biopsy, tumor

DIAGNOSIS:
Brain left parietal lobe, biopsy: glioblastoma multiforme (astrocytoma WHO grade IV)

CLINICAL DATA:
The patient is a 50-year-old woman with a left parietal lobe lesion, probably GBM

TISSUE, GROSS DESCRIPTION:
The specimen is received in two parts from operating room 4, each labeled with the patient's name and medical record number. Part A, received fresh and additionally labeled "I – tumor (FS)," consists of a single, delicate tan fragment measuring 0.4 x 0.3 x 0.3 cm. Small portions are used for touch preparation and frozen section diagnosis 1, with the frozen section remnant submitted in cassette A1. The remainder is submitted in A2. Part B, received in formalin and labeled "2 – tumor permanent." Consists of multiple soft, irregular pieces of pink-red tissue measuring 1.3 x 0.9 x 0.3 cm in aggregate. The specimen is entirely submitted in cassette B1.

INTEROPERATIVE DIAGNOSIS:
Brain, left parietal lobe, biopsy: Strongly favor glioblastoma multiforme, presence of eosinophilic granular bodies includes PXA with anaplasia in differential. Tissue section and cytologic preparation.

COMMENTS:
This glioblastoma multiforme shows extreme cytoplasmic and nuclear pleomorphism with occasional giant cells. Abundant mitotic figures are present, as are multiple foci of necrosis. Scattered eosinophilic granular bodies are present.

PATHOLOGIST:
Bollen, Andrew W., MD

CHAPTER FIFTEEN

Recovery Room
Nighttime, Thursday, April 6, 2006

Late the night of my surgery I am moved from recovery to the floor. "Which floor will I be on?" I ask.

"You'll be on the surgical floor."

"What floor?"

"Fourth floor."

Fourth floor, I repeat to myself, hanging onto the words. "I was on the eleventh floor. Will my family know where to find me?"

"We'll let them know."

Jack and Jennifer are already in my room when I am wheeled in. Once the attendants leave, I sit up. "Hey. I am so happy that's behind me." I turn to Jack. "Did you see Dr. Berger?"

"We did. I'll never forget it. He was standing outside the elevator drinking a bottle of water. He took a swig and said, 'I got it all.' Slurp. 'I got it all.' It was amazing. He was so confident."

"We got a phone call about every hour," Jen says.

"From whom?"

"Somebody from the operating room. Jen's right. We got an update about every hour. And then I'd call your mom and my sister, and they would call everyone else."

> **FACULTY**
> **Department of Neurological Surgery**
>
> Mitchel S. Berger, M.D., Chair
> Director, Neurological Surgery Research Laboratories

"See the picture I took," Jen says.

I examine her digital camera and see that she has taken a picture of tall, double glass doors. Above the doors are the words *Department of Neurological Surgery*. Painted on the glass are the names of the UCSF neurologists and neurosurgeons. Dr. Berger is listed at the top: Mitchel S. Berger, M.D., Chair.

"Wow," I say.

"We got the top guy," Jack says. "He thinks he got it all. He kept repeating that. He was so confident. But he also said there will always be a chance that one tiny cell remains, so they will follow you closely for a while."

"I can do that. Wow," I say again. "We didn't know we were asking for the chief." I swing my legs over the side of the bed.

"Wait," Jack says. "Are you allowed to do that?" I slide off the bed and set my feet on the floor.

"Shouldn't you have socks on?" he asks.

"Too slippery." I untangle the IV lines and grasp the IV pole.

Jack grabs my elbow. "What are you doing?"

"I'm going to the bathroom. And yes, I'm allowed to." I shuffle the several steps from the bed to the bathroom door, holding my hospital gown closed at the back and towing the IV pole along in my wake. "I'll be right out."

When I emerge, both Jack and Jen are hovering near the bathroom door.

"Does it hurt, Mom?" Jen asks.

"Not at all."

"Get back in bed," says Jack, propelling me by the elbow across the floor.

"Okay," I say.

We are still together when the floor nurse appears. "Well, we have a roomful here. How are you feeling?"

"I'm fine," I answer.

"Let me see that wristband. Tell me your name."

"Doree O'Connell."

"Date of birth."

"October 30."

"Where are you?"

"UCSF Medical Center, fourth floor."

"Actually, you're on the eighth floor."

"No, I'm on the fourth floor."

"Eighth floor."

"Fourth," I insist.

The nurse regards me with surprise. "You're right. I'm usually on the eighth floor, but I'm covering the fourth floor today."

Jack shakes his head. "You haven't lost a step."

"Good one, Mom," says Jennifer.

If they only knew how frightened I've been of losing my memory, I think, and how hard I've tried to remember.

"And why are you here?" the nurse continues.

"I had a brain tumor."

She notices my use of the past tense. "But no more."

"No more."

"No more," Jack echoes.

The nurse nods her head, a matter-of-fact acceptance of my statement. She checks fluid levels in the IV bags, smoothes tape at the IV sites, and straightens bedcovers. She studies the electronic graph that monitors heart rate and blood pressure, reaches out and adjusts a knob, then turns to Jack and Jennifer. "Just a short while more," she says. "It's been quite a day."

"Quite a day," Jack echoes.

I look at Jack, hear him bid the nurse good night, watch him pat Jennifer's arm, and remember the life I had imagined as a young girl. I wasn't going to marry. Not ever. The oldest of five siblings, I was responsibility personified, and I was looking beyond the walls of my home, around the corners of my hometown, across the globe. I wanted the independent life of an independent woman. I wanted to travel.

My plan was a little seed that I had planted somewhere in the course of my youth, and it germinated and bloomed through a humanities course, through art appreciation and music classes, through four years of French. I wanted to live in Europe. But Europe was too far away, too expensive. I wrote to the Canadian Department of Tourism and requested brochures on jobs, housing, even the economy, which I pored over by the light of a flashlight under the bedcovers at night in the bedroom I shared with two sisters.

I would live in Quebec, I had decided. I would work as a waitress in a coffee shop where I would practice my French, absorb the culture, and write wonderful essays from the point of view of an expatriate living abroad, essays that were witty and charming and full of pithy observations. I would develop friends who were cultured and musically inclined and who would spend their free hours browsing through art museums with me.

All this, though, was practice—the opening act, if you will—for moving to France. Ah, France, the land of my dreams: the world of evenings spent at outdoor cafés drinking coffee in cups the size of thimbles, gesticulating wildly while discussing the writings of Rousseau and Proust, falling madly in love. He would be a poet, ride an old two-wheeler, and wear a beret. Our lives would be meaningful and relevant and heartfelt.

And that was my plan. But, like most plans, things didn't go as scripted. And while I was busy working, studying, and dreaming of my future, life happened. That particular night at work I stood lost in thought at the counter I was polishing, absently moving the cloth back and forth across the glass surface, Eve waiting for her Adam. When he spoke behind me, I was ready for him. And he wasn't Adam, just a handsome young man with unruly brown curls above warm chocolate eyes. There was something in the way he looked at me, and into me, a simple acknowledgment of two souls connecting: "Why, there you are." There was something solidly dependable about him, a kind of innate strength and self-confidence and sense of safety. I had an urge to smooth back the shock of brown hair that fell across his forehead.

As I write this, thirty-nine years have passed. I've never waitressed in a coffee shop, nor lived in Quebec. I study Spanish now, and my travels have taken me to Mexico, not France. My friends today are no less cultured or interesting than those in my make-believe world, but discussions of poetry have been replaced by debates of politics and current events. My husband suffers through art museums, preferring instead the excitement of a rock concert or an NBA game, and the bicycle he rides stays firmly planted on our bedroom floor. He has never worn a beret, nor read Rousseau or Proust, and I struggle to write essays that are witty and charming and full of pithy observations. Yet together we raised a beautiful daughter, poured our souls into causes we believe in, laughed at the same jokes. We've supported each other through the loss of loved ones, through career changes, through lengthy commutes or moves to different communities, and now he is supporting me through this.

"It's been quite a day," Jack says again.

"Quite a day," I echo, and suddenly, like a deflated balloon, my energy is depleted.

"Time to go," Jack says.

I grab his hand before he leaves. "I love you," I say. "Both of you. See you in the morning."

CHAPTER SIXTEEN

First Day of the Rest of My Life
Friday, April 7, 2006

It's Friday, my first day post-surgery, and Ted is my first visitor. A former legislator and Jack's Sacramento roommate, Ted has remained close friends with Jack. Several years and three children earlier, Jack had officiated the wedding of Ted and his wife, Nicole. "Daddy married Ted," a young Jennifer was fond of saying. It is good to see him.

My sister Leslee and brother-in-law Tom drive over from the Central Valley. "Mom wishes she were here," Leslee whispers as she gives me a hug.

"Tell her I'm fine and I'll see her in a couple days," I whisper back.

Cheryl arrives armed with a heavy, silver-toned vase filled with fresh-cut flowers. "You know me; I couldn't come empty-handed," she said.

"It looks old."

"I found it at a thrift shop on my way here. I liked the heft." She pumps the vase up and down as if working out with weights. We both laugh. "Jennifer was great," Cheryl adds. "She had your cell phone and was calling a few key people. I just thought, 'Oh no, not Doree! Not Doree!' I had to come see you for myself."

I swallow hard and blink back tears of disappointment. "I don't know about Italy," I finally say. "And I keep thinking of Theresa." A mutual friend of ours, Theresa had her life irrevocably altered when she suffered a ruptured brain aneurysm two years earlier. Near death and in a hospital for months, Theresa survived, but her severe brain injury destroyed her short-term memory; the outcome was life in a memory care facility.

"Me too," Cheryl says. "Me too. But you're not Theresa. And Italy will still be there. The important thing is that you're here, and you're talking, and you are you. Thank god," she adds.

"I'm here. Still not quite sure what happened, but I'm here."

"You're in the newspaper, Mom," Jennifer says.

"What newspaper?"

"Lots of them."

"Why?"

Jack is apologetic. "It's my staff," he says. "People were calling. I've missed a lot of appointments, canceled speeches. There were rumors."

"People thought something was wrong with you?"

He nods. "So we put out a press release. We didn't say much," he hastens to add when he sees my face. "But it got picked up on the wire service, so it's pretty much in most of the papers. I'm sorry."

I'm quiet for a moment, absorbing the news. I like my anonymity. I like the fact that when I meet people who don't know Jack, or don't know my relationship to him, they meet me as me. Not as Jack's wife, not as the wife of an elected official. Just Doree. It's an important distinction to me. It's allowed me to live a private life, to know those people who are true friends and to recognize those who are more impressed by status or title.

Still, I can't fault Jack, and considering the last few days, I cannot give that simple act more power than it's worth. "No more stealth wife," I say.

"No more stealth wife."

On Saturday, my sister-in-law Nancy arrives. She flies from Los Angeles to support her brother and niece and fills the air with chatting and jokes, lunches in the cafeteria with them, and takes Jennifer shopping at the University of California, San Francisco bookstore across the street from the UCSF Medical Center. I learn this later when Jennifer hands me a stuffed teddy bear. The bear wears a shirt that reads "Somebody at UCSF Loves Me."

The day passes with a gamut of emotions: euphoria, relief, depression, gratitude, anxiety, euphoria again. I'm not sure how much of this is due to medication or to the fact that I've gone through brain surgery, though I suspect it's probably a combination of both. I'm offered pain medication, which I decline, not because of a fear of being sick again, but rather because, though my head feels fragile, as if I am balancing a ball on top of a pole, I have no pain whatsoever. I am amazed, especially considering the debilitating headaches I suffered before surgery.

IV bags drip fluids and steroids into my veins, the fluids to hydrate me, the steroids to reduce the swelling in my brain. Thanks to the constant influx of fluids into my system I am out of bed frequently, towing the IV pole in the crook of my right arm while holding the gown closed in the back. On about the third trip, I am aware that the nurses have relaxed their vigilance, which makes me feel capable and strong.

I drift in and out of sleep, then wake to a dinner tray being served. The food seems heavy, too solid for my digestion, but I manage to swallow hot tea and Jell-O, spooning up the latter with my left hand. My right hand, still weak and without sensation, cannot form a fist. I think about the things I'll need to relearn if it doesn't improve: brushing my teeth, combing my hair, writing.

My blood pressure and temperature are taken frequently, and a couple medical students wander in and out of my room, eager to ask questions and jot notes of my replies in the large medical charts they all carry. I learn then that Dr. Berger, who had been scheduled to teach the day of my surgery, instead had his class observe my surgery from a high, glassed-in room. It's clear to me that the students feel vested in the outcome.

My hand drifts often to the side of my head where I finger the horseshoe-shaped curve of staples. I feel a single staple lower at the back of my head and wonder at its purpose and how it got there. I pick small, sticky round sponges from my chest, hip, and underarm, remnants of the monitors attached to me during surgery. I'm edgy and tense and need to remind myself to breathe and to feel gratitude. The lights in the hallway remain constant, and I am aware that night has fallen only when the hospital room grows dim.

I struggle out of the sheets, swing my legs over the side of the bed, grip the IV pole and tow it behind me to the bathroom. Thanks to an innovative nurse, a second hospital gown I now wear backwards functions as a bathrobe, and I no longer need to hold the back closed behind me.

The voices in my room tell me that Jack, Jen, and Nancy have arrived to say good night. I hear water running in the small sink outside the bathroom door, and when I emerge, I note that Jack has scrubbed his hands with antibacterial soap. I appreciate his desire to protect me from germs but groan at the splashes of water along the edges of the sink. "Just like home," I say, grabbing a handful of paper towels to mop up the water. "This is not a hotel, you know."

Nancy laughs. "There she is."

I grin sheepishly at Jack, briefly ashamed for my scolding, then turn to Nancy. "Oh my god, Nancy, I had a brain tumor. I'm still trying to wrap my mind around it." I turn to offer her my profile. "I had my head cut open. See the staples?" Nancy moves closer to examine the side of my head.

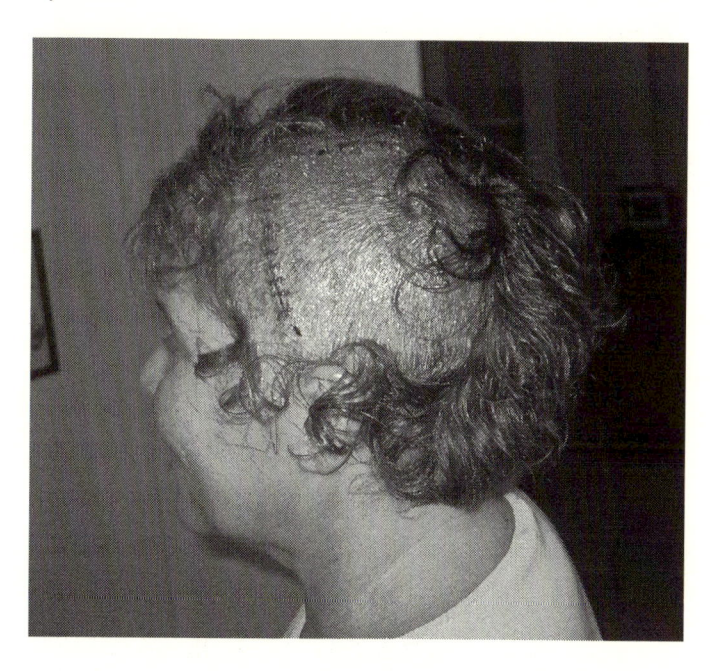

"I still say you look like you've been kicked in the head by a horse," Jack says.

A nurse enters the room in time to hear his comment and joins us in our laughter. "I'll let you visit a little longer," she says as she leaves.

"Well, I can go home," says Nancy. "I just had to see you for myself."

A sudden thought occurs. "Uh-oh," I say, and turn to Jack. "Uh-oh."

"What?"

"I made a complete mishmash of the checkbook this month." I cringe, remembering my struggle to write the monthly bills. Why didn't I see then that something was wrong?

"We'll figure it out."

"I guess I was trying so hard to make things work that I couldn't stop to acknowledge I was having trouble. Why did I do that?"

"Who knows why? The brain is a complex organ."

"And my brain wasn't letting me accept something was wrong." I lie back, suddenly overwhelmed and exhausted. "I don't know if I even got the checks in the right envelopes."

"It's okay," Jack says.

"I couldn't hold on to things. I kept dropping them. At the pool. In the kitchen." A sudden thought occurs. "I couldn't enter student ID numbers in the computer at work. I'll have to fix that. Numbers didn't make sense to me. Nothing made sense."

"It's okay," Jack says again. "Tomorrow. We'll deal with it tomorrow."

CHAPTER SEVENTEEN

Out!
Sunday, April 9, 2006

I want out. I want out of the hospital, and I want to go home, and I want to take a shower, but my IV has leaked. My arm is huge, filled with fluids that missed the vein and settled into the tissues in my arm. I lie flat, arm elevated on several pillows to help the fluids absorb into my system, mad at myself because—in a determined effort to ignore the irritating tape, the bruises, the dull ache of the IV needles—I never notice that my arm is nearly three times its normal size.

Nurse Terrence is doubtful I will be released today. "We release patients in the morning," he says. "You'll be here into the afternoon, so we may keep you overnight."

"No," I say.

"We might."

"I can go home today."

He ignores me and asks the familiar litany of questions: name, birthday, date, location. "Who's our president?" he asks, throwing me a curve.

"President?"

"Of the United States."

I'm grumpy, tired of being the obedient patient. "Do I have to say his name?"

Terrence laughs, a loud release of noise.

"Are we kindred spirits?" I ask.

"I believe we are," he says, and we talk San Francisco politics long enough to charm me out of my funk.

"I'll be back," he says.

"I'll be here." As the door swishes closed behind him, I add under my breath, "And I'm going home today."

It's mid-afternoon when the hospital agrees to release me, but as a condition of my release I am required to stay in the immediate area overnight. "Just to be sure," Terrence says. "Will you stay in a San Francisco hotel tonight?"

I look at Jack, who nods his confirmation. "Daly City all right?" he asks Terrence. "It's a twenty-to-thirty-minute drive."

"Good enough. Let's get the paperwork done, set you up with a couple prescriptions and a medication schedule, and get you on your way."

And finally, after an amazing four days, I'm out and breathing cold, fresh air. I recline against the front passenger seat and gingerly tuck two hospital-issue pillows behind my neck. Though I feel every crack in the road, I'm elated to be out.

Our first stop, a few blocks from the hospital, is Walgreens Drugstore to fill prescriptions. Days earlier, in a meeting with a UCSF medical resident, I signed papers agreeing to join a clinical trial for Keppra, an anti-seizure drug. The young doctor spoke earnestly about science and side effects and knowledge certain to aid the medical community. I listened in snatches, aware that my brain was having difficulty tracking his words, but felt empowered to be asked to participate. A second prescription is for Decadron, a steroid. It's my hope that the month supply will be all I need and will include a period of weaning off that drug. I know the steroid is necessary to reduce continued swelling in my brain, but I suspect that drug to be the cause of my feelings of anxiety and the reason why I now sleep in two-hour increments.

When Jack and Jen emerge from the drugstore, Jen proudly shows me the seven-day pillbox she bought me. I'm impressed with her thoughtfulness but at the same time flash on a memory of watching my seventy-six-year-old mother counting out a two-week supply of medication and vitamins for her pillboxes. Will this be my life?

Jen's cell phone rings on our drive to the hotel. Her friend Daniel, who has driven to UCSF to support her, can't find us at the hospital. Jen and Jack give him driving directions to the hotel in Daly City, but the directions are confusing and beyond my grasp, so I stop listening. All I can think about is a bath.

Jack escorts me down the long hotel hallway, his hand firmly under my elbow. "You get your own room tonight," he says.

"My own room?"

"So you can sleep. I know it's hard to sleep in a hospital."

Anticipation of being able to bathe overwhelms any doubts I have about being left alone. "Fine," I say.

Jack bustles around the hotel room, drawing curtains tight, turning down the bedcovers. "Okay?" he asks.

"Okay," I say. And finally, I'm alone, seated on the edge of the tub watching steam rise from hot water pouring from the faucet. I unwrap a new bar of soap, uncap the small bottle of shampoo, and stack towels at the edge of the tub. And then I'm in the water, chills running up my spine, and all is right with my world. I use a washcloth to scrub half my head, leaving the surgery side dry and untouched. It will be another week before I am allowed to stand under a shower. I soak until the water has cooled and the antiseptic stench of hospital is washed away. And then I empty the cooling water and fill the tub again, reclining in hot water until my skin is blanched and wrinkled. I think of Jennifer as a little girl banging on pots and pans while splashing in warm, soapy water in the kitchen sink. I wonder if this is the same kind of joy she felt.

Out of the tub, I rummage through my clothing choices—jeans, T-shirt, jacket, clogs—the same items I wore to the hospital a lifetime ago. I select the T-shirt and gingerly pull it over my head, stretching the neck to avoid the staples. I wrap a clean towel around my waist and sit on the edge of the bed, arms dangling. Even if I can find a comb, I am too tired to brush my tangled hair.

I hear a knock. "Dor?"

It's Jack, but the level of anxiety in his voice is unfamiliar.

"Doree?" he says again.

"Coming." I push myself up and will my limbs to move.

"Is everything all right?" he asks when I click open the hotel deadbolt.

"I'm clean. I feel good. What's up?"

"I'm staying here tonight."

"I wondered."

"Yeah, Nancy called, chewed me out when she heard I'd put you in your own room."

"She's right."

Jack sits on the bed next to me. "I just wanted you to have a good night's sleep."

"I will, but someone should stay."

"That would be me," Jack says. "Just don't tell her I let you take a bath alone on the day you're released from the hospital."

"I'm not thinking clearly either."

"Jen and Dan found an In-N-Out Burger. Do you want anything?"

"Did I eat today? I don't think I did." And suddenly, I'm starving. "A hamburger. And a carton of milk."

"Are you sure?" Jack asks. "That doesn't sound like you."

"I'm sure."

Jack stands. "I'll go tell them." He hesitates, his hand on the door. "On second thought, I'll call them, have them bring it here."

"You just don't want me to tell Nancy on you."

Jack grins. "One chewing out a day is enough."

CHAPTER EIGHTEEN

Discharge Summary
April 9, 2006

DISCHARGE SUMMARY

ADMISSION:
April 6, 2006

DISCHARGE:
April 9, 2006

DISCHARGE SERVICE:
Neurosurgery

DISPOSITION:
Home

HISTORY OF PRESENT ILLNESS:
This is a 50-year-old woman with no significant past medical history who was transferred from an outside hospital presenting with 3-4 days of word-finding difficulties and also right arm paresthesias. Work-up at the outside hospital revealed a 3 cm left parietal mass with surrounding edema and 5 mm of midline shift from left to right on CT imaging.

PAST MEDICAL HISTORY:
Significant for cesarean section

MEDICATIONS:
None

ALLERGIES:
Penicillin, rash

SOCIAL HISTORY:
Married, no illicit drug use

PHYSICAL EXAMINATION:
The patient was afebrile with vital signs stable. She was alert and oriented x3, following commands, with good language function and no signs of aphasia. Naming and counting were intact. Her cranial nerve examination was intact. She did have a right pronator drift on the right upper extremity. She had decreased sensation in her right upper extremity as well. Reflex examination was normal. Her gait was within normal limits. MRI revealed a left parietal lesion with 5 mm of midline shift and surrounding edema.

HOSPITAL COURSE:
The patient was admitted to the Neurological Service at UCSF. Given her symptoms, the patient was worked up for her brain metastasis, including a repeat Stealth MRI as well as chest and abdomen CT scan. She was also started on steroids to reduce her intracranial swelling. During her work-up, it was discovered that she had an 18 cm pelvic mass. The Gynecology Service was consulted. They thought this was consistent with a fibroid, but a malignancy could not be excluded.

Given that she was symptomatic from her intracranial tumor, however, she was taken to the operating room on 4/6/06 for left parietal craniotomy and resection of tumor using Stealth neuronavigation and motor mapping. The patient tolerated this procedure well and postoperatively was observed in the intensive care unit.

Postoperatively, she has some subtle decrease in strength in her right grip with apraxia. Her language function was intact with fluent speech. This weakness in her grip improved over time. The remainder of her hospital course recovery in the ward was uneventful, and she essentially recovered to the point of her preoperative neurologic status.

The Gynecology Service continued to follow her throughout the course of her hospitalization. They recommended an outpatient endometrial biopsy. The patient will follow up with the gynecologist attending and was instructed to call 885-7788 for a follow-up appointment. This was in order to rule out malignancy, given, however, that her pelvic mass would most likely be a fibroid.

Once all of this work-up was completed and she had a good recovery from her craniotomy, the patient was discharged to home in excellent condition. She will follow up with Dr. Berger in our Neuro-Oncology Clinic within 2–4 weeks. Her staples will be removed in 10–14 days

DISCHARGE MEDICATION:

1. Decadron taper
2. Keppra 1000 mg p.o. b.i.d. as part of the KEPDIL Study
3. Dexamethasone taper
4. Vicodin
5. Pepcid
6. Colace

ATTENDING MD:
Berger, Mitchel S., MD

CHAPTER NINETEEN

Home
Monday, April 10, 2006

Our travel day dawns wet and stormy. My head feels fragile, so Jack drives with care, avoiding all bumps in the road that he can. Jen and Daniel leave early with the intention of arriving first to clean the house and set up the downstairs bedroom where I'll sleep until permitted to climb stairs, but roads are slick and travel slow, so they arrive home just before we do. I'm content to rest on the couch while my room is readied. Missy, our golden retriever, leans against me and lays her head in my lap. I stroke her and think about how intuitive animals are.

TC, my walking friend, visits and shares news of baby goslings and ducklings born in the creek that winds along our favorite path. "I hear squawks too," she says, referring to the great blue herons that nest high in eucalyptus trees that line an open stretch, "but I can't see the babies yet."

Cheryl visits too. "I can't believe you drove to UCSF to see me in the hospital," I say. "Especially since I just did it in reverse. It's a long drive, and you came through the rain too."

"I had to see my travel buddy."

"I don't know what will happen," I answer, referring to more than our Italy trip. "Bad timing."

"Bad timing," Cheryl agrees. "But let's not give up yet. When do you have a follow-up appointment? I assume it's with the doctors at UCSF?"

"It is. Ten days. I'll know more in ten days. Right now, I'm euphoric. I mean, my head was cut open. And I survived. You know how people say, 'It's not brain surgery?' Well, this was. Dr. Berger believes he removed the whole tumor. I want to know what kind it was. I need to go online, research it. Of course, the tumor was biopsied after surgery, so I'll get those results when I'm back for my appointment with Dr. Chang in ten days." We're quiet for a moment, each with our own thoughts, before I venture, "It must be benign. Don't you think? Benign?"

"It must be. You're so healthy. It must be."

"A blip on the radar," I say, hoping with all my might that it is. "A blip on the radar."

It's once again a bath that motivates me to climb the stairs to the large tub in the master bedroom. This time Jack accompanies me and seats me on the bed while he runs the water. "Stay there," he says, but I'm anxious for the steamy water and don't obey for long.

"That looks good," I say at his elbow. "Let's put some bubbles in."

"Didn't I tell you to stay there?"

"I'm not going to fall over. Besides, I have to regain my strength, so it's good to be up. Can you reach that bottle?"

He stretches across the tub with his long arm, snags the soap bubbles, uncaps the bottle, and adds some sweet-smelling pink soap to the rapidly rising bath water. I watch the solution mix with water pouring from the faucet and sigh in anticipation.

Jack smiles. "Okay. Call me if you need help."

I smile back. "I won't."

Days pass fast. Thoughtful neighbors bring too much food; too many bouquets of flowers are delivered. Friends Teri, Teri's sister, Sharon, and Coleen bring pizza and salad from Nucci's for lunch. Talk revolves around recent current events, and I'm struck by the knowledge that a month ago I could talk politics with them, but today words swirl in abstract plays of color and bright light. I don't have energy enough to explain to them how their words elude me. I smile and laugh and chew on a slice of Thai chicken pizza, normally a favorite, but now too heavy for my stomach. I love having them here, but when they leave, I am exhausted with trying, afraid my brain will never work again.

In the beginning, Jack shields me from the barrage of phone calls. Soon, though, I acknowledge the benefits of vulnerability and openness. I didn't choose to telegraph my illness to the world, but letting go of privacy allows me to experience the outpouring of love and concern, and soon I insist on answering the phone myself.

Jack's office sends me a large box stuffed with cards and letters sent to my attention at the Department of Education. Like a child at the school carnival fishing booth, I sift through the treasure chest and pull out small gifts: an angel, a prayer bracelet, an anointed cloth, a Native American fetish. I use the simple act of writing thank-you notes as my own personal form of physical therapy for a right hand that is slow to recover.

I walk at dark with Jack and Missy. The nights are cool, so the beanie I wear to cover the staples in my head does not seem out of place. My normal even-keeled temperament is missing, though, replaced by emotional jags that fluctuate between euphoria and despair. I laugh and cry and don't recognize myself. Steroids, I think. This is what steroids do to the body.

Sometime during the ten-day wait for my appointment in San Francisco, a nurse from UCSF calls to request the name and address of the referring doctor from Sierra Vista Hospital. "We would like to send him the surgical report and keep him apprised of follow-up appointments."

"Sure," I say. "His name is—" and then I stop, unable to remember. "It's—, it's—"

"I see the name Dr. Segal mentioned in the records. Was he the doctor you saw at Sierra Vista?"

Relief floods through me. "Yes. That's it. I was drawing a blank on his name. Segal, Dr. Segal. That's it."

"You wouldn't happen to know his address, would you?"

"I can get it for you." I pull a phone directory from the cupboard underneath the phone. "Give me just a second. I'll look him up." I open the phone book. "Segal, Segal—" I thumb through the white pages, in *F*, then *P*. Where is he?

I'm searching through *D* for Doctor when she interrupts my search. "It's all right. I can look him up. I just thought maybe—"

"No, no. I can get it for you." *A, B, C, D. S.* Where's *S*?

"Try the neurology listings in the physicians section of the yellow pages," she says. "Find neurology, then look for Dr. Segal's name."

Yellow pages. I flip through the book to the yellow pages. Neurology. *P*? Is that one of those medical words that sounds like *N* but is spelled with a *P*?

"It's all right," she says again.

"No," I say. "It's not." Is *P* before *N*? "Why can't I find this?" A movement in my peripheral vision catches my attention. It's Jack, sprawled on the floor in front of the TV, oblivious to my distress. I watch as he tucks a pillow under his head and flips the channel between ballgames. "Jack."

Jack sits up. "Is it for me?"

"Help," I say.

"Who is it?"

"It's a nurse at UCSF."

"Does she want to talk to me?"

"I need you to talk to her. I can't answer her question."

"Okay." He grunts up from the floor, glances at the televised ballgame, walks towards the outstretched phone, but it's not until he sees my face that he knows I'm upset. "What's wrong?"

"I can't find Dr. Segal in the phonebook. Help her, will you?" I hand Jack the phone and, without a backwards glance, climb the stairs to splash water on my face.

CHAPTER TWENTY

Dr. Chang's Diagnosis
Wednesday, April 19, 2006

I remember the day my cousin Michael died. I remember Aunt Bev's voice on the phone when she told me how he had been playing a neighborhood game of football, that he'd gone long for a pass, pumping his legs as hard and fast as an athletic fourteen-year-old can do, that he collapsed on the field just as the football sailed on the wind over his head. I remember how I hung up the phone and how, in a rational, almost clinical way, I conveyed the news to my dad. It wasn't until the next day when I knelt on the driveway at Michael's home in a neighboring town to help his little brother that realization hit. "Tsoos," Joey said, pointing to red, snub-nosed sneakers on the wrong feet, oblivious to my tears. "See?" he said, pointing at his feet as I bent low to switch the shoes and retie the laces. "Tsoos."

Ten days are up. Jack, Jennifer, and I drive north. A forced gaiety, helped in part by the fact we are also bringing our friend TC with us, masks anxiety.

Coincidentally, two months earlier, TC had enlisted my help to drive her to a scheduled surgery at Seton Medical Center in Daly City, just south of San Francisco. The fact that we can see the hospital on a hill rising above the city from our hotel room is fortuitous, since Jennifer will be the one to drive TC to her appointment early the next morning and me home after that. Jack has a plane ticket to Los Angeles in his briefcase. He will travel to L.A. immediately after my appointment this afternoon to attend a ceremony honoring his sister, Nancy, as a teacher of the year for her school district. After thirty years of marriage, though, I understand him. Even if he didn't have this event scheduled, an event that we both want him to attend, he has no room to absorb any more. Whatever the news is that we are destined to hear, he'll stay on schedule. That's Jack.

"Do you want to come with us?" I ask TC after we all check in at the hotel. "You don't really want to hang out at the hotel by yourself all afternoon, do you?"

"I'll wait. You go. You should do this together."

"I don't mind. And I expect good news."

"No, I'll stay here. We'll have dinner together tonight." She stops, then asks, "Are you ready if the news isn't good?"

It's a thought that has been with me the past ten days, flitting through my head like a hummingbird in flight, its glittery wake leaving a trail of unease. Will I hear bad news? How will I handle it? What will it mean? What will I do? Will I be clinical, detached, as I was that moment long ago when I learned about Michael, or will I fall apart?

~~~

The cramped office at UCSF Medical Center accommodates us, but barely. Dr. Chang sits at a computer, its screen turned to display 130 images of my brain. It looks like a walnut, I think. Cross-section slices from a walnut. Dr. Chang talks as she flips through the views slice by slice. "There are over 120 different types of brain tumors," she begins. "They can be benign or malignant, and sometimes benign tumors can cause more serious health problems because of where they are located. We use the World Health Organization classification system to identify brain tumors, and we assign them a grade ranging from grade I, or least malignant, to grade IV, which is usually an aggressive and fast-growing malignancy."

Dr. Chang's scholarly lecture flows around me, through me. I hear words but cannot grasp meaning, so I study the computer screen and attempt to glean information from the pictures. On the pre-surgery side of the screen I see the tumor. It appears as a soft blob, round and white. The post-surgery side of the screen offers the view of a cavernous, fluid-filled dent in my brain where the tumor once lodged.

"Each person, each tumor, is unique," Dr. Chang is saying.

"Is it malignant?" I blurt out.

"Your particular tumor originates in the glial cells of the brain," Dr. Chang explains. "An astrocytoma is a glioma that develops from the star-shaped glial cells called astrocytes that support nerve cells. Yours is a grade IV astrocytoma, which is also called a glioblastoma multiforme, or GBM. And *multiforme* because of the wide variation in the size of the cells."

She continues to talk, but I see a sudden paleness to Jennifer's skin, see her wide and startled eyes, and I forget to listen. I think of my mom's friend Beth and my cousin Marilyn, both of whom succumbed to brain cancer shortly after their diagnoses. I know what GBM means, the course that disease takes. I know my prognosis is grim.

It's not true that at times like these one's life flashes before one's eyes, at least it didn't for me. Instead, my head fills with a roar so great that thoughts can't penetrate. I can't form the words, can't see the image, but the understanding that I have brain cancer courses through my veins. I grope for the box of tissues on Dr. Chang's table. Turns out, I didn't need to worry about being clinical and detached after all.

Wow, I think. So this is what it's like to be told that your life as you know it is over. My life will never be the same. I will never be the same. I am different. People who came before me, who sat in this chair and heard these very words, are changed. I view the scene from a distance somewhere beyond my right shoulder, see the middle-aged woman dabbing her eyes with a tissue, the beautiful young woman with a deer-in-the-headlights look on her face, the tall man in suit coat and tie, his head cocked, a slight pucker between his eyes as he concentrates on the words spoken by the tall, slim Asian woman in a white doctor's coat.

Dr. Chang is discussing treatment options when Jack interrupts. "Wait a minute," he says. "You didn't answer Doree's question about whether the tumor is malignant or not."

Jennifer and I answer with one voice. "Oh yes, she did."

"She did?" Jack asks, clearly puzzled. "What did she say?"

"I know what GBM is," I say to him. "It's brain cancer."

The room is silent. "You're kidding," Jack finally says.

CHAPTER TWENTY-ONE

Fifty with a Vengeance
Thursday, April 20, 2006

The bed frame creaks every time Jennifer thrashes her legs or rolls over to punch the hard hotel pillow into a yielding shape for her head. I'm not sure if her restlessness stems from concern for me or anxiety that she will sleep through her alarm and be late getting TC to the hospital early next morning. I suspect it's a little of both.

I, on the other hand, am barely breathing. My physical stillness belies the chaos in my mind, my thoughts swirling, almost incoherent. I am glad Jack is not with us; I am not ready to talk. I wish Jennifer had gone with him, wish she were out with her friends, wish for her to be anywhere except this hotel room, but I need her to drive me home. It's a relief for both of us when, finally, the light gray of early morning seeps through the part in the hotel curtain.

Jen and I talk surface talk all the way home. We are both still stunned by yesterday's news, both still holding it at arm's length. I want to be home, to be in safe, familiar surroundings where I can shut the door on a world that is changing too fast. My mom's car, though, is parked in the driveway when we arrive home.

Last night from my hotel room I had called her, dreading the news I had for her, though I delivered it in a calm and assured voice. "It's cancerous," I said, avoiding the word GBM. "It *was* cancer," I amended, "but the surgeon got it all. I'll have to go through treatment, radiation, and chemo, but that's just a precaution. He got it all," I assured us both.

She was more matter-of-fact, this woman who had lost her husband and two sisters to cancer, than I gave her credit for. "Then we'll fight hard," she said. "And you are strong."

I resolved then and there that, if possible, I would outlive my mother. "Children, no matter how old they are, should never predecease their parents," I said to Jennifer after I hung up. "You keep that in mind."

Jennifer skillfully maneuvers the car into the garage and parks. "Home, Mom."

I echo her. "Home." In the house I stroke Missy, grateful for her wise brown eyes and gracefully waving tail, grateful to feel her warm length lean against my leg. I holler hello and follow the sound of my mom's voice upstairs, where I find her scrubbing away her worry in my shower.

Later, I think about how naïve I am to believe I'm in control of my life, that if I plan the journey and work hard, life will go according to plan. But does life ever go according to plan? I should know by now it never does.

At twenty, I am engaged to be married. Jack is a high school teacher, a life I understand well. After all, I was raised by two teachers. But does he stay a high school teacher? No, he does not. Instead, he becomes an elected official, a lifestyle I know nothing about.

Jack and I talk about children and agree on zero or two; neither of us wishes to saddle our child with only-child status. I am thirty when we are blessed with the birth of our daughter, and though she is the most significant love in our lives, she remains an only child.

I dream of college, of meaningful and important work as a journalist, or maybe a forest ranger, but I leave school early to marry and turn instead to a career as a court reporter. It's not until I reach forty that I return to Cal Poly to finish my degree.

And cancer? Definitely not a part of the plan.

Today, at fifty, I'm struck by the knowledge I haven't accomplished nearly all I hoped to by this time in my life. I haven't traveled or learned a second language or lived in another country. Nor have I mastered the piano or learned to paint. And I haven't published a novel. A half a century has passed; fifty years are gone. Where's my plan now?

The afternoon finds me seated at the computer. I have news to share, but how can I ever begin to express how I feel? I flex my hands, drum my fingers on the desk, and begin:

> Dear family and friends,
>
> I turned fifty with a vengeance! Most of you know what happened to me over the span of the last two weeks, from a week of migraines, to hearing the words "inoperable brain tumor" in our local ER, to a miraculous surgery at UCSF. Well, there's more. I've been sitting here in front of the computer trying to think how best to tell you my news, and I flashed on a conversation I had with my father eight years ago. It went something like this:
>
> "Hi honey." Pause. "Give me a minute." Another pause. "I've been practicing saying this to you kids all day." Swallow. "I've got cancer."

Well, I've been practicing too, and the words don't come out any easier. The pathology report confirmed our worst fear, that the brain tumor was a cancerous mass. Not only that, it's a particularly nasty, aggressive, fast-growing form of brain cancer that probably grew within the last six months. Treatment starts soon: radiation and chemo for as long as I can tolerate it, which I intend to. The surgeon felt he removed 100% of the tumor, so I am starting from a good position, but we all know someone who has battled cancer in the past or who is currently fighting the good fight today, and I know I'm in for it.

So here's what I need to say: this past week has been incredible. I have felt so loved, from neighbors delivering gifts of food, friends carrying frozen yogurt and DVDs, and the visits and myriad of phone calls from family and friends. You've been wonderful, but it's time for me to roll up the welcome mat and retreat. Please don't be upset with me for feeling like I need to self-focus. This significant event in my life has happened so fast that I am having a hard time wrapping my mind around the magnitude of what I am facing. No more gifts of food—I'm on a special diet as of today—but emails are grand, and phone messages are appreciated. And I promise that eventually, within the next couple of weeks, I'll even pick up the phone and return your calls.

Thanks for your support, for your love, for your concern, for your prayers. I've heard every whispered plea and accept them all. Those of you who know Jack and Jennifer, hold them close. They're reeling too.

~~~

I am ignoring the phone, but when I hear Jack's voice on the message machine later that evening, I answer. It's a measure of our comfort as husband and wife that we don't waste time on niceties. "Where are you?" I ask.

"Sacramento."

"How'd it go today?"

"Good. Glad I went." He pauses. "Everyone is talking about your email. It's well written."

"It's from the heart."

"That too." Another pause, then, "I need to come home." I hear the strain in his voice, an unfamiliar sound. Unflappable Jack is more inclined to joke his way through a serious discussion than show his feelings. In fact, I've seen him cry only a few times in our life: Jennifer's birth, the deaths of both our fathers, life's main events. He dons his blinders and plows through his daily schedule. Level-headed common sense guides him, not emotion. But it's emotion that I hear now.

"Then come home," I say.

"I should."

"You should. Let someone else give the speeches for a few days."

"They've been doing that all week."

"They'll understand," I say. "Come home. We need you. You need us."

I hear the emotion again in his voice. "Have Jen get me at the airport?"

"At whatever time."

"I'll call when I land."

"See you then." I disconnect and stretch out on the family room couch, leaving the phone within easy reach.

CHAPTER TWENTY-TWO

The Low Point
Saturday, April 29, 2006

Life settles into an uneasy routine. After a few days of respite at home, Jack resumes his duties at the Department of Education. Jennifer, who suspended her cosmetology school program the day I went to the hospital, goes job hunting. I am left alone to heal. I spend anxious, distracted days pondering odd bits of Buddhist literature, New Age writings, and poetry. I read two newspapers a day, puzzle over the daily crossword, and spend too much time researching online cancer websites. In the evenings I cover my half-shaved head with a knit cap and, with Missy my eager companion, wander through the neighborhood, breathing crisp night air and thinking. Friends visit or call, and I talk. I'm in "wait" mode: waiting for the treatment schedule from Dr. Chang, waiting for the go-ahead signal from the radiologist, waiting for my first round of chemotherapy, waiting, waiting, waiting.

I know one thing I must do, though I dread it, so one quiet weekend morning I pick up the phone. "Cheryl?"

"Doree. Oh, it's so good to hear your voice. How are you?"

"Better than I expected to be. How are you? How's school?"

"Winding down. We're doing oral presentations the next two weeks, and then a paper, and then we're in finals week," Cheryl said, referring to her teaching position at Cuesta Community College. She pauses. "And then Italy."

"I hate what I have to say."

"I know."

"Don't you dare say Italy will still be there."

"I would never say that."

"I want to go now, and I want to go with you."

"Me too," she says, and suddenly we are both crying.

"Best-laid plans and all that," I say, wiping my face.

"Best-laid plans," Cheryl agrees.

Later that morning I stretch along the length of the couch and absently thumb the pages of a favorite novel. I peer over the book, then lay it across my stomach, distracted by a baseball game on TV. I watch a play, then another before I pick up the book to resume reading. I read a page of words but my attention drifts, and I set the book down again. The cool spring gloom outside matches my mood, and tears sting my eyes.

Earlier in the week, I'd felt so buoyed by the support of family and friends that I had sent out a second email loaded with assurance that I would beat this disease. Today, though, worry is a thick blanket of heavy fog, suffocating me, and the questions won't be denied. Will I be able to handle the chemo? Will I lose my hair? Will I be a burden to my family?

Sitting up, I wipe my eyes on my sweatshirt sleeve and drag my laptop toward me. Maybe if I catch up on emails, I'll feel productive and my mood will lift. But as I sift through my emails, it's my own words, those upbeat words from five days ago, that draw my attention:

> Dear family and friends,
>
> Thank you for respecting my need for space. I can't even begin to express how frightening it was to hear the words "malignant brain cancer." We've needed this week—all three of us—to mourn what we've lost and to reorganize our thinking about how different life will be this next year. We *were* right to retreat, though,

because today we feel stronger emotionally and ready to do battle. Guess it's all a part of the process.

Jack and I have been married for nearly thirty years; for twenty-four of those, he's been in public office. And for those twenty-four years I have prided myself on my ability to skate under the radar and protect my anonymity. In fact, the big joke in our family is Jack's nickname for me: stealth wife. And this is one of the reasons why dealing with such a private trauma in such a public way has been especially difficult for me.

Now having said that, I must also share that I've learned true life lessons this month: how to let go of the external and focus on the internal; how to allow oneself to be vulnerable; how to let people help, something this fiercely independent woman has never had to do; and how, when I do all of the above, I will experience such a heartfelt outpouring of love and support I've never experienced before in my life.

Here's what I know:

Jack and Jennifer are awesome, and I am truly blessed.

I have *the* best support system of family and friends *ever*!

I had *the* best neurosurgeon the world had to offer, a pioneering giant who said, "We had a total resection of the tumor," and, "I got it all." I hold on to those words as I begin round after round of radiation and chemo, because they mean that my starting line is ahead of the gate.

I may eventually die from brain cancer, but not today. In fact, I'm shooting for a decade!

There's more, but I push the laptop away, stare out the window at the gray April skies.

"You'll go to Italy someday." Jack's voice comes from behind my head.

I nod. "I know. It was just a low point."

"You've never been to Europe, but we've gone other places. Hawaii. The Bahamas."

"The Cayman Islands. Cabo."

"New York. Chicago. Boston."

"Boston was amazing," I say.

"Don't forget Washington, D.C. That was a great trip."

"Catalina," Jack says, and I smile my first smile of the day.

"Catalina time," we say in unison, and suddenly I'm back in Avalon.

In my memory, the boat's engine rumbled, a constant backdrop. It punctuated laughs from upper-deck tourists and quiet conversations of locals seated at inside tables and hunched over Styrofoam cups of black coffee. Large Costco and Wal-Mart bags, reasons for the mainland visit, bounced and vibrated against the cabin's plastic benches. I felt the rumble through my shoes and in my bones as I leaned against the deck railing, straining for that first glimpse of Santa Catalina Island's rugged cliffs rising from a navy sea twenty-six miles off the coast of Long Beach, California.

"Did you change your watch yet?" my husband asked.

I looked at him blankly.

"Your watch," he said patiently, holding out his wrist for me to see. "Don't forget the forty-minute time difference."

Catalina time, a phrase we've coined during our years "overseas," as Jack calls our jaunts to his favorite island, defines our island visits: simpler, slower, broken into easy components of walking, eating, sleeping, and walking again.

"It's Catalina time," I say now to Jack. "That's the mind-set I need." Book forgotten, ballgame ignored, I close my eyes and dream.

CHAPTER TWENTY-THREE

Dr. Stella
Wednesday, May 3, 2006

Jack and Jennifer go with me to my first appointment with radiologist Dr. Jonathan Stella. It's been one month since surgery, two weeks since diagnosis, but it seems I've been waiting months to be here. I am anxious to start treatment, whatever it might be.

Jen has her arm linked through mine, and I take a deep breath as I approach the front desk.

"Hi," I say. "I have an appointment."

"Name?"

"O'Connell. Doree O'Connell."

The nurse is all business. "Did you bring in the documents we sent you?"

"Oh. Yes. Right here." I hand over the packet I'd filled out a week earlier.

"And I'll make a copy of your insurance card too."

I pull my wallet out of my purse, extract the card, and hand it to her.

"Thanks. And while I'm making a copy, this is a form giving us permission to bill your insurance, and this is a copy of our privacy policy." She points. "We need your signature here and here."

Paperwork completed, Jack and Jen flank me as we settle into chairs in the sunny waiting room. Jack and Jen talk; I try not to stare. I am amazed at how comfortable the other patients are with their baldness, how colorful and cheerful their assorted hats and scarves are. This is surreal, I think. And that's not me. I hear the conversation that swirls around me but don't listen and instead read ads posted on the waiting room wall for wigs and volunteer drivers for cancer patients. That's not me, I think again. How did Dad do it? What was he thinking during all the medical appointments those last two years of his life? My mind shies from reality, from the radiologist's waiting room and baldness covered with brightly colored scarves, and instead follows the trail to a happier memory, a time outdoors in nature, a time when I was young and fishing with my dad.

"Are you sure?" he had asked then. "Let 'em go?" Gone was the father who had patiently untangled my fishing line from my brother's, the man who had baited our hooks, the gentle dad who had gotten our lunches out of the cooler at ten thirty in the morning when we were sure it was lunchtime. He lifted up the eight trout, attached by chains he had threaded through their gills to keep them alive in the clear mountain water. They were beautiful: rainbow-hued and glinting silver in the sun. "Are you sure?" he asked again.

Camping trip, summer of 1966: Navajo Lake in southern Utah sat at 8,500 feet, surrounded by a dense forest of aspen and ponderosa pine. The weather-sculpted limestone formations set against the red sandstone towers and deep canyons were spectacular. This alpine lake that the Native Americans called Blue Mirror of Heaven was icy—pure melted snowpack. Heavy clouds scudded low over the lake and wrapped around the mountains. It had rained for days. The big blue tent stood stalwart, its soaked and sagging canvas dipping towards the middle. Mom told us not to touch, but we couldn't help it. The warmth of our fingers against the inside of the canvas tent drew water in and down, a steady drip of condensation and rainwater into the center of our living quarters. Dad had dug trenches around the outside of the tent to prevent the water from flowing up and over our zippered doorway and ponding inside.

Dad and my brother David, age nine, sat in the tent and talked about the fishing they'd do when the weather lifted. Fish and Game kept the lake stocked, mostly young rainbow trout and cutthroats, but David was after the big fish—the "natives"—that hung low in deep, quiet pools snug against rocks and upended roots of fallen trees.

"I'm gonna sneak up so they don't see me. I'll lie down on that log and put my reel over the top. They'll never know what hit 'em."

Dad just laughed. He understood this firstborn son of his, so like himself. Eight-year-old Leslee, Dan, six, and Toni, five, were absorbed with make-believe games. At eleven, I was the oldest and Mom's right-hand girl.

"I'm the mom," Leslee announced. "You're the dad." She pointed at Dan. He bounced, recognizing a new game. "I'm also the princess," Leslee continued, nodding her tousled head for emphasis.

"But I want to be the princess." Toni's bottom lip quivered.

"You can't," Leslee said. "You're the baby."

"Oh, let her be the princess," I said.

Dan studied me for a moment. "Yeah, she's in a castle, and I can climb up and rescue her. I'm Batman."

My mom looked at me. "How about another game of cards?"

I sighed. We'd read stories, told jokes, sang the theme songs to favorite television shows, and played I Spy so often that we all knew where the one yellow item in the whole tent was—the zipper pull on Dan's jacket. I was tired, and besides, the deck of cards was wet and stuck together like sticky, wet cardboard.

That night the storm broke, and my spirits rose with the ever-lightening slashes of pink and orange in the eastern sky. The day dawned, a perfect deep-blue canopy dotted with cauliflower clouds that stretched overhead. The tent was thrown open, and the sleeping bags were set to air in the sunshine. Mom, armed with broom and towels, bustled between the picnic table and tent.

"You got those three?" my dad asked her. The three little ones, decked out in sweatshirts and brightly colored rain boots, played at water's edge, digging with sticks in mud, gathering rocks, and resuming the previous day's game of Batman Saves the Princess. "I'm taking these two fishing." Dad folded down the back seat of the old white station wagon, loaded it with our lunch cooler, his tackle box, his hip waders. He pushed his arms through the armholes of his multi-pocketed fishing vest, tossed in his old Zebco rod for me, David's pole, and the spinning reel he'd been waiting days to use. The reel mechanism hung off the bottom of the pole. I remember Dad liked that because it was more sensitive than a top reel. He could hold his finger against the line as it ran out the reel, along the length of the pole, and out the tip. He could feel when he had a fish on the line.

Fishing: the great tradition in my family. As for me, I preferred sitting on rocks in the middle of streams, feeling the sun prickling hot across my back and shivers rippling up my arms from trailing hands in icy water. I enjoyed the quietude, the peaceful daydream world that belonged to me alone. In the music of the wind bending through trees and stirring the water, I could hear voices of the ancients whisper their message of man and time.

So there I spent my day, lost in solitude, all the while casting off, reeling in, and casting off again, which is why my father spent most of his day pulling hooks off moss and lines out of trees and untangling my line from my brother's, and which was also why my avid fisherman father had not caught a single fish, and I had caught eight. He stood before me and held up the rainbow trout attached by chains he had threaded through their gills to keep them alive in the clean mountain water. "Are you sure?" he asked me again. "Let 'em go?"

The summer sun had dropped below the distant hill, and long fingers of leaf-filtered light dappled through trees and around rocks, then faded. The evening was silent and empty. The air was cool. The scent of pine had evaporated with the light. He read my answer in my face.

"Hello." The arrival of the tall and boyish Dr. Stella, an athletic-looking forty-five-year-old with a mop of brown hair and a calm demeanor, interrupts my daydream. He is sympathetic, but not overly so, for which I am grateful. I can handle the clinical tone better. I learn that I'll start with radiation five days a week for six weeks, coupled with a daily dose of an oral chemotherapy drug called Temodar.

"When can I start?" I ask.

Dr. Stella smiles. "Not yet. You need a mask. We'll set up a time for you to meet our technician, Dale, at San Luis Diagnostic Center to make your mask."

"Mask?"

"It's a sheet of plastic mesh that we dip in hot water to soften and make pliable. You will lie on the MRI table while it's molded to your face. During your radiation sessions, we'll snap it to the table to hold your head still."

"My own mask?"

"Molded to your face."

"Snapped to the table?"

"To keep your head still. We want to zap only specific areas in your brain, not the whole brain."

I look at Jack and Jennifer, trying to picture this.

"Anything else I should be asking?" Jack asks Dr. Stella. "How does it work? The radiation, I mean."

"It's actually called stereotactic radiotherapy, which uses computer imaging to precisely locate the tumor area. Radiation works by damaging DNA, which stops cells from dividing. When the tumor cells that received radiation try to divide, they'll die. It's a low dose of radiation administered over a period of time to specific pinpoint areas." Dr. Stella turns to me. "And that's part of the process of making the mask. You'll be snapped to the table while Dale creates a computer program specific to you."

"How much radiation does this use?" Jack asks. "I mean, I'm sure it will affect her."

Dr. Stella nods. "It's a low dose, and these doses do add up over time, but it's the only way we can safely treat areas of the head without harm to the eyes, or the optic nerve, or the brain stem."

"Will I be able to drive?" I ask.

"We can line up friends," Jack says.

"Actually," Dr. Stella says, "you should be able to drive yourself to all your appointments. Have you driven since your surgery?"

"No."

"I didn't see in the records that you had seizures."

"No, no seizures."

"Do what's comfortable for you, and that includes drive yourself if you want. That's okay."

"Will I feel it?" I ask, my mind back on the radiation treatment.

Dr. Stella shakes his head. "You'll hear a quiet hum, but you won't feel it. You'll feel tired, though," he adds. "Fatigue is one of the side effects." He pauses. "Another side effect is you'll lose your hair."

"I will?" I ask. "Really?"

"I'm sorry to tell you that, but yes, you will."

"From the chemo?"

"No. From the radiation."

"The radiation?"

"From the radiation. And only on half of your head."

I groan. "Half of my head?"

Dr. Stella nods. "And you may have other side effects to look forward to. We talked about fatigue and hair loss. You may have loss of appetite or some nausea, but because you will be taking anti-nausea drugs daily before you take the Temodar, you may not notice those symptoms. But memory loss. Problems with thinking and reasoning. Loss of coordination." Dr. Stella ticks off the possible side effects on long, tapered fingers.

I am mesmerized by the flow of words and the accompanying hand movements until I'm jerked back to the present as Jack and Jennifer stand up.

I've already got cognitive problems, I think, and I haven't even started yet. This isn't good.

CHAPTER TWENTY-FOUR

Radiation and the Mask
Friday, May 5, 2006

My energy level is at low ebb, and though Dale is gentle and kind, tears drip down my face throughout our meeting at San Luis Diagnostic. Molding the plastic mask is not difficult and feels more like warm towels draped across my face than any kind of medical treatment. But when I'm snapped to the table for the length of time it takes Dale to program the computer to be able to direct beams of radiation to the tumor area, I cry again. I try to steer my thoughts away from where I am, away from the mask on my face and towards friends and favorite childhood memories, to my silent vow to not predecease my mother. Finally, Dale marks radiation points on the now-hardened plastic mask with an indelible marker, unsnaps the mask from the table, helps me sit up, and hands me the tissue box.

"We're set," he said. "I'll take the mask to the office. We'll keep it there during treatment so you don't have to worry about bringing it back and forth. Your pills have been ordered and should arrive through the mail in a couple days. You will start those the same day you start radiation."

"When?"

"Next week. Five days a week for six weeks."

"Okay," I say.

The following week I arrive early for my first radiation treatment. I don't want to spend more time than necessary in the doctor's office, so I decide instead to wait in the car. I straighten my head scarf, reapply lip gloss, check my cell phone to be sure it is turned off, and wait for the exact moment of my appointment.

"Coastal Radiation," I read. The letters are in script, painted in white on the clear glass doors. I breathe deeply before I push my way inside.

In the treatment room I am instructed to lie on a narrow gurney, so narrow that I feel like I need to tuck my hands under my hips to keep them from dangling off the sides. The technician explains that once I'm set up, she will leave the room and communicate with me through the intercom system.

"You'll hear me, and I'll hear you, but I can't be in the room. See this?" She fingers a badge attached to the front of her scrubs.

"That's different-looking."

"This measures the amount of radiation I am exposed to." She holds up a warm blanket and raises her eyebrows. At my nod, she tucks it around me. "I have to scan the badge every day to be sure I'm not getting too much radiation."

"Do you worry about that?" I ask.

She shakes her head. "Not really. We are always careful." She points to a wide window adjacent to the heavy metal door. Beyond the window is a desk area with scattered papers. "I'll be there. And my badge has always registered minimal radiation levels." She reaches for my mask and holds it up. "I'll snap you in, and then I'll leave for about five minutes. You won't feel a thing."

True to her word, I hear a noise similar to the hum of a dental X-ray machine. But whereas that noise in the dental office lasts but two seconds, the hum I hear now is continuous. I visualize the beam directed at my head and worry that it's destroying healthy brain cells. Will this work? Will it make me sick? Will I live? I battle the impulse to wrestle my way out of the blanket tucked around me, fight the urge to rip the mask from my head, taste tears. When the technician finally unsnaps the mask that pins my head to the gurney, the rising panic in the pit of my stomach threatens to level me.

She grasps my shoulder to help me up. "It gets easier," she said. "You'll see."

In the ensuing weeks, friends and family offer car rides and company. I am grateful, but I drive myself to every appointment alone. It's personal, and I try to explain to them how important it is to me to feel a semblance of control over my life. I am worn out, worried. I alternate between feeling empowered and anxious. Soon I stop crying through my radiation appointments. Soon, too, I am not startled every time I see the waiting room filled with illness, though I continue to view myself as separate from that. Afternoons find me at home dozing in a chair, an open book in my lap. I start many books in those six weeks but never finish one.

It's not until the third week of radiation that my hair begins to come out—first, long strands on my pillow in the morning, then clumps in the shower. I am surprised by how painful it is. Within a few days, half my hair is gone. True to Dr. Stella's prediction, I have a perfect part down the center of my head, from brow line to the base of my skull. Oddly, a one-inch fringe running along the nape of my neck from ear to ear remains.

"Help," I say one day in early June to Jennifer. "I need a haircut. Can you cut the other side really short? Cut it as short as possible. All that hair under the scarf makes my head look lopsided."

"Sure," she says. "All of it? Should we shave it?"

"No. See this fringe down here?" I finger it. "I've discovered that when I wear a baseball cap, it looks like I actually have hair. See?" I don the hat and model for her.

"Oh, yeah."

"Look what else I've got. A doo rag."

"Doo rag? Like for under motorcycle helmets?"

I grin. "Or bike helmets." I put the blue kerchief cap on my head. "See? It's already tied behind my head and has a little tail hanging down in the back."

"Cool," Jennifer says.

"It works great under a baseball cap too. I ordered more, but I need this hair cut off first."

"And I went to cosmetology school for this," Jennifer mutters.

On my last scheduled day of radiation, Dr. Stella hands me my mask. "A souvenir for you," he says.

"Will I have to use it again?"

"I hope not. In fact, I hope never again. But with this type of tumor we never know." He pauses. "I know you've been reading about GBM, so I know you understand there is an average life expectancy of nine to fourteen months after diagnosis, and that's with treatment. Everyone is unique. I have a GBM patient now, and she's still going strong after two years. But we will worry about a recurrence when it happens."

"How about if it happens."

Dr. Stella is somber. "Okay. I'll give you that. *If* it happens." He clears his throat. "You have your follow-up MRI with Dr. Chang at UCSF scheduled?"

"Next week."

"Good. Be sure I am on the distribution list. I want to read all the reports. You have a lull in your treatment now, about a month. Now is the time to take care of the mass in your abdomen that was discovered during your work-up for brain surgery."

I nod. "It's a fibroid. But I will."

"Dr. Chang will talk to you about a possible hysterectomy at UCSF."

I nod again. "I'm looking forward to it."

At his sudden grin I add, "No. Really. I *am* looking forward to it. And then I'm done with surgeries."

"We certainly hope so."

"Will I see you again?"

"I'll have you make a couple follow-up appointments so I can see how you are progressing. We'll check your gait, your speech, your eyes, your hand strength, but no radiation. The thing about radiation is that you may experience negative effects in your brain long after the treatment is finished, so we'll monitor you for a while. You will continue with the Temodar, which I can continue prescribing for you, but you really should start treating with an oncologist. Do you have an oncologist yet?"

I grimace at the word. "Not yet. Do you have someone you recommend?"

"I do." Dr. Stella takes a business card out of his wallet and scribbles a name on the back. "Tom Spillane. His office is over by French Hospital. You'll like him." He offers his hand, and I take it. "Take care," he says.

CHAPTER TWENTY-FIVE

Chemotherapy and Dr. Spillane
Tuesday, July 18, 2006

My first appointment with Dr. Spillane comes a week after my hysterectomy, and for the first time I call a friend for a ride.

"Let's go to lunch first," Coleen says. "There's a new crepe place in town."

I laugh. I'm a week out of the hospital after having abdominal surgery, but lunch with Coleen sounds good. "Why not?" I ask.

Dr. Spillane's waiting room is similar to Dr. Stella's: cheerful and sunny, and the comfortable chairs that line the wall are filled with a sea of scarves, hats, and wigs and peppered with an occasional bald head. That's not me, I start, but stop short, and my happiness at being out to lunch with a friend deflates like a balloon. That *is* me. I am at an oncologist's office. Coleen senses my change in mood and starts a lively chat. Her distraction helps.

Dr. Spillane is young, and his head is clean-shaven. His eyes are direct, his handshake firm. I like him instantly.

"Do you have anyone with you?"

"I came with a friend. She's in the waiting room."

"She can come in if you'd like her here."

I shake my head. "No, I'm fine."

"Glioblastoma multiforme," Dr. Spillane says, checking his chart before glancing at me. "How did that happen? You look amazingly healthy for someone who just went through brain surgery, what, three months ago?" He checks the chart again. "How did you know to go to the hospital? What were your symptoms?"

"Terrible migraine, or at least I thought it was a migraine."

"Do you get migraines often?"

"I've never had a migraine. I just thought that must be what one feels like."

"And how's that?"

"Debilitating and painful. And then I started doing funny things: dropping a glass, tripping up a curb. I couldn't picture numbers, couldn't put them in order. I even put my keys in the refrigerator. I just turned fifty, and I blamed my symptoms on menopause."

"How about now? Any headaches?"

"None. My head sometimes feels a little fragile, like I'm balancing it on my neck, but other than that, no headaches."

"Let's have you lie up here on the table," Dr. Spillane says, patting the examination room table. I obey, but when I lie flat, I groan as I feel abdominal stitches stretch against tight skin.

"What's the matter?" Dr. Spillane asks as he reaches out to grab me. "What hurts?"

"You're going to have to help me up when we're done. I have no stomach muscles. I had a hysterectomy a week ago."

"Hysterectomy?"

"Hysterectomy. I've had a bad year."

"I'll say. How do you feel?"

"Rescued."

He laughs at my answer, and I like him all over again.

Before I leave Dr. Spillane's office that day, I know my treatment schedule: five days of the oral chemotherapy drug Temodar every twenty-eight days, anti-nausea pills twice a day during the week of treatment, a daily antibiotic, a blood test at French Hospital once a month the week before treatment to check blood-count levels, an appointment once a month with Dr. Spillane to check lab reports and order the next month's pills, and MRIs every two months.

"For how long?" I ask.

"For as long as you can tolerate it."

~~~

Life settles into a pattern. Jack commutes weekly to Sacramento, leaving Monday morning and returning home to San Luis Obispo on Thursday or Friday evening. I spend my days reading or visiting with friends and family. I answer emails from other GBM patients and families who reach out to me; we share encouragement and information with one another. I hide feelings of sadness, of how overwhelmed I am by my diagnosis. I wonder if my personality has changed and if others notice. At dark, Missy and I wander the neighborhood, and I'm grateful for her solid presence at my side as I think about life and death and work to regain my energy.

My high school friend Jeanne shows up for our lunch date in a baseball cap to match the one I wear, and I laugh when I see her. We vow to keep our lifetime friendship alive. My museum friend, Donna, meets me for breakfast and gifts me with a book of poetry. I vow to read every poem. My sisters, Leslee and Toni, visit for a weekend. We talk, share medical research articles, and stories of hope and courage. I know they are afraid for me.

My strength begins to return, and I am able to resume a moderate walk twice a week with my walking partner, TC. We delight in watching downy ducklings take their first plunge into the creek along the path that leads to Avila Beach, watch them swim with an instinctual knowing, watch the parents protect and encourage.

I retreat to the safety of home for chemo weeks, anticipating illness, but except for mild symptoms, the nausea and fatigue I expect never fully materialize. I soon learn how to maneuver the week of chemo by eating a light diet and resting often. I forget to take my anti-nausea medication only once during what will eventually be twenty-two months of chemotherapy; the ensuing twelve hours of violent illness is an effective deterrent to any further lapses in attention.

During this time period, I meet a kindred spirit in the form of Ann, a resident of San Luis Obispo and brain cancer survivor extraordinaire. She lives a quiet life, a life nonetheless filled with art, music, yoga, meditation, and organic vegetables from a garden lovingly tended by her husband, Jim. I am heartened by the fact that her diagnosis came five years before mine. She has outlived her prognosis. I feel less alone.

CHAPTER TWENTY-SIX

California Department of Education
September 2006

One day in early September, Jack approaches me with a proposition. "We're planning our department-wide meeting," he says, referring to the annual gathering of one thousand California Department of Education employees at the art deco Crest Theater in downtown Sacramento. "We have the usual skits and speeches planned and a very talented street artist named Garibaldi for the entertainment, but I wonder if you'd like to come address the crowd."

"Me?"

"Yeah. You always said you were so appreciative of all the cards and gifts everyone sent. I can't go anywhere in the department without someone stopping me to ask how you are. I think it would be good for people to see how well you are doing. And it would help me too."

"What would I say?"

"Anything you want. Even just thank you."

"Can I think about it?"

"I won't say a word. I won't even tell the guys at the department that you might come. You can be a surprise guest. We'll sneak you in the back door."

"Okay," I say. "I'll let you know."

Two weeks later I travel to Sacramento with Jack, and on the morning of the department-wide meeting, I enter the back door of the theater and find a dark corner in the wings offstage to watch the show. I pace, stop to listen, pace some more. I rub my hands, take swift, shallow breaths, stop to listen again. Jack has prearranged with me the moment where I will appear; I know the exact sentence in his speech where I will climb the short flight of stairs and enter, stage left.

But my cue never comes. Suddenly, I am aware of a deep silence, a silence that hangs heavy in the stuffy theater air, a silence that stretches like the taut string of a violin until it snaps, broken by a sound: a sob. A voice catches. Someone struggles for words, pauses, tries again. The audience is as still as night. Before I even form the conscious thought that that's my husband out there and he needs rescuing, I'm climbing the stairs and crossing the stage. To this day, I don't know if the thunderous applause is for Jack or me. I suspect it's a little of both.

"Hi," I begin. "I'm Doree O'Connell. I see some familiar faces in the audience, but most of you I don't know on a personal level. I feel like I do, though. I always believed that Jack's success in the legislature and as a teacher stemmed from the fact that he surrounded himself with bright, engaged, caring people. And I'm here to tell you that I can personally attest to the fact that the Department of Education is no different."

Jack pats my back when I stop to clear my throat. "Um, these past few months have been a roller coaster of emotions, but always, when I seemed to be at a low point, something arrived in the mail from the department to cheer me up, to help me feel connected to the larger picture, to feel a part of the family."

I take a deep breath. It's silent in the theater. "Mark Twain once said it usually took him more than three weeks to prepare a good impromptu speech. Um, well, I've been thinking about you folks for months now, wondering what I'd say to you if I ever had a chance to speak personally to you. And simply, it's this: thank you. Thank you to all of you who wrote to tell me you lit candles for me or added my name to prayer lists. And to those who sent emails, anointed cloths, flowers, angel pins, and

Native American fetishes: thank you. I figure they represent different paths leading to healing, and I am grateful for them all. I am truly humbled by your heartfelt words and caring support."

It's my first-ever standing ovation.

CHAPTER TWENTY-SEVEN

Nutritional Advice

At some point during my journey, I attended a conference on brain tumors in Sacramento. The information I received was valuable, and the sheer amount of information presented was tremendous. I was brain-dead by the end of the day, pun intended.

The presentation by the nutritionist was especially interesting to me, because she addressed exactly what I had been researching. I wanted to follow an anti-inflammation diet and had found information in that regard from Dr. Andrew Weil and Dr. Nicholas Perricone, to name two sources, and what they wrote coincided with what I heard at the conference. The nutritional bottom line was that eliminating inflammation and regulating blood sugar levels prolonged survival and increased effectiveness of the body.

Maxine Barish-Wreden, MD, ABIHM, a holistic/integrative medicine specialist, directed her talk to preventing brain cancer in particular, but said throughout the presentation that what she had to say related to anti-inflammation and anti-cancer diets as well. She said that cancer researchers agree that 80–90 percent of all cancers are related to the environment, including quality of food, obesity, and inactivity.

According to Dr. Barish-Wreden, the most important goals in any healthy eating plan are to reduce inflammation, maintain normal blood sugar levels, support the immune system, and keep one's body as lean and fit as possible. She linked chronic inflammation to cancer, arthritis, diabetes, and Alzheimer's, among other diseases. Between 1950 and 1999, incidences of cancer were up by a rate of 80 percent in all industrialized countries, so many of the herbs and supplements she recommended were from Asian and East Indian cultures.

Nutritional recommendations:

- Restrict animal foods, especially commercially raised meat, poultry, dairy, and eggs; eliminate dairy completely if at all possible;
- Increase intake of fish, especially omega-3 cold water fish, wild only;
- Increase soy protein foods (a controversial opinion);
- Limit intake of omega-6 fatty acid vegetable oils, including corn, sesame, peanut, and canola; safflower oil is okay, olive oil is superior, and grapeseed oil is best for high-temperature cooking;
- Increase dietary antioxidants by raising intake to 8–12 servings per day of deeply pigmented organic fruits and vegetables; the brighter or deeper the color, the more nutrients there are;
- Eliminate refined carbohydrates, such as all white foods like sugar, white flour, white rice, and potatoes; use whole grains only, and don't get caught in the trap of thinking that whole wheat flour is a whole grain;
- Increase the use of healing herbs and spices in cooking, including herbs such as turmeric, garlic, and ginger; the more herbs used in cooking, the better;
- Drink green tea regularly, approximately 3–6 glasses a day;
- Avoid fruit juices because of their high sugar content;
- Avoid artificial sweeteners and preservatives at all costs; and
- Eat 35–50 mg of fiber daily; this is easy to do when you eat beans, legumes, brown rice, steel-cut oatmeal, grains, and Ezekiel bread.

Supplement recommendations:

- Increase omega-3 fatty acids such as fish oil, with a goal of 2,000–3,000 mg per day of EPA/DHA;
- Take a vitamin D3 supplement (cholecalciferol) with an optimum dose of 1,000–2,000 IU per day (confirm dose with a blood test for vitamin D level);
- Add a multivitamin every day, one that includes the RDA for zinc, magnesium, selenium, vitamin C, niacin (vitamin B3), and pyridoxine (vitamin B6); be careful with vitamin A as it is toxic in large quantities; and
- Consider taking other supplements under the care of a health professional, such as boswellia (Ayurvedic herb), bromelain (from pineapple), melatonin, curcumin (the Indian spice turmeric), quercetin (found in citrus), and ginger.

Other recommendations:

- Optimize blood sugar control;
- Reduce stress;
- Get plenty of sleep;
- Engage in daily moderate activity;
- Consider guided imagery or meditation; and
- Find something you love to do—and do it often.

Resources:
Jeanne M. Wallace, PhD, CNC, www.nutritional-solutions.net
The China Study: The Most Comprehensive Study of Nutrition Ever Conducted and the Startling Implications for Diet, Weight Loss, and Long-Term Health by T. Colin Campbell, PhD and Thomas M. Campbell II
Nurture Nature, Nurture Health: Your Health and the Environment by Mitchell L. Gaynor, MD
ConsumerLab.com

CHAPTER TWENTY-EIGHT

UCSF Medical Center: MRI Report and Letter
March 9, 2007

UCSF MEDICAL CENTER: MRI Report

PT NAME: O'Connell Doree J.
SEX: F
REPORT STATUS: Finalized

PROCEDURES: MRI brain unenhanced and enhanced (3-9-07 11:30)
MRI OF THE BRAIN: 03/09/2007
COMPARISON: 01/10/2007

CLINICAL HISTORY:
51-year-old female with history of glioblastoma multiforme, status post resection, for interval follow-up.

TECHNIQUE:
Following a multiplanar localizer, the following sequences were obtained: Axial FLAIR, coronal FLAIR, sagittal T1 spin-echo, axial T1, axial T1 post-gadolinium, coronal T1 post gadolinium, axial FLAIR, coronal FLAIR.

FINDINGS:
As compared to previous study, there have been no significant interval changes. There is again evidence of prior left parietal craniotomy with underlying resection cavity. There is extensive FLAIR hyperintensity around the left parietal and left posterior frontal region, unchanged in appearance. There is also mild linear enhancement identified along the posterior margin of the resection cavity, which demonstrates no significant interval change.

There are no new foci of enhancement of FLAIR signal abnormality.

The ventricles and sulci are within normal limits. The orbits appear grossly unremarkable. There is a mucus retention cyst versus polyp seen within the right maxillary sinus.

Diffusion-weighted imaging reveals no evidence of reduced diffusion to suggest acute ischemia.

The bones are grossly unremarkable.

IMPRESSION:
When compared to previous study of 01/10/2007, no significant interval change, with no new FLAIR hyperintensity or enhancement.

RADIOLOGIST:
Mukherjee, Pratik
Wilson, David

ORDERING MD:
Chang, Susan

UCSF MEDICAL CENTER: Letter

PT NAME: O'Connell, Doree J
SEX: F

Department of Neurological Surgery
400 Parnassus Avenue Eighth Floor, Box 0372
San Francisco, California 94143-0372 Tel: (415) 353-7500
Fax: (415) 353-2167
Neuro-Oncology Service

March 9, 2007
Thomas Spillane, MD
1941 Johnson Avenue, Suite 201 San Luis Obispo, CA 93401

Service date: 03/09/07

Dear Colleague:

We saw the patient in the Neuro-Oncology clinic on March 9, 2007. As you know, she is a 51-year-old, right-handed female with a left parietal glioblastoma. She has completed approximately eight cycles of adjuvant Temodar therapy without significant side effects. She complains of only mild stomach discomfort with Temodar and some mild fatigue that are easily managed. She feels functionally more independent. She has no complaints currently. Her current medications currently include only prophylactic Bactrim.

On physical exam, her KPS score is 90. She is in no apparent distress. Her pupils are equal, round, and reactive to light and accommodation. Her extraocular muscles are intact. Her oropharynx is clear. Her neck is supple without lymphadenopathy. Her chest is clear to auscultation bilaterally. Her heart has a regular rate and rhythm with a normal S1 and S2. Her abdomen is benign with normal bowel sounds, soft, nontender, and nondistended. She has no cyanosis, clubbing, or edema. She has a well-healed craniotomy scar.

On neurologic exam, she is alert and oriented to time, place, and person. Her memory, attention span, concentration, language, and fund of knowledge are all within normal limits. Her cranial nerves II-XII and visual fields are within normal limits. Her sensory, strength, tone, coordination, gait, and reflexes are all within normal limits. An MRI of the brain on March 9, 2007, compared to an MRI of the brain on January 10, 2007, shows no change in the FLAIR signal. There is no new enhancement noted.

In summary, this is a 51-year-old, right-handed female with a left parietal glioblastoma who is clinically and radiographically stable on adjuvant Temodar. She will continue her Temodar therapy at this point and initiate her next cycle this evening. She will return to the clinic in two months after her next MRI scan. Her questions were answered, and routine precautions were given. Thank you for allowing us to participate in the care of this patient.

Sincerely,
Raymond Liu, MD
Susan Chang, MD

CHAPTER TWENTY-NINE

Financial Issues

Nobody ever told me how financially stressful cancer is. When I was first diagnosed in April 2006, my health took center stage. From the moment I stepped foot in the emergency room at French Hospital until I underwent brain surgery two days later at UCSF, events happened at warp speed. I accepted the path that I was on and never questioned the wisdom of the decisions made for and around me.

There is a reason doctors tell patients small bits of information at a time, and it's because in that moment of chaos, when one's world spins out of control, we patients are capable only of baby steps.

"We're sending you by ambulance to this hospital; they have better MRI equipment." Then, "We're sending you to that hospital; there is a brilliant surgeon there." And, "Tests today, surgery tomorrow; come back in ten days for the biopsy report." I did what I was told—mostly—and didn't ask the hard questions.

The reality was I needed those early days to adjust, to wrap my mind around the fact that I had had brain surgery, and to relish the euphoria that I had survived. "It must be benign," I said often in those early days. "Look at me. I'm the most robustly healthy person I know." I don't know what would have happened if, while I was in the recovery room, someone said to me, "You have GBM, the fastest-growing and most malignant of over 120 types of brain tumors." Would I have just given up?

I'd like to think I'd be able to accept the news and, with strength and understanding, calmly discuss with the doctor what I needed to do to regain my health. But who knows?

The bill for my hospitalization and surgery arrived shortly after diagnosis. Already reeling from learning I had brain cancer, the bill for $100,000 stunned me. Though Jack and I had good health insurance, it didn't cover all. By this time in the process, I had begun to read more online articles about GBM, absorbing all I could learn about the disease I faced and its grim survival rate. I began to worry about money. How would I pay my medical bills? MRIs scheduled for every other month were costly. How could I pay those bills if I were going to be dead in nine to fourteen months?

Determined not to saddle Jack with medical expenses, and unbeknownst to him, I took out a life insurance policy that did not require a doctor's exam. I wanted Jack to have enough money to bury me. A few months later, the state of California again was unable to pass its budget, and, as in past years when the state was without a spending plan, Jack's paychecks were suspended. I liquidated two IRAs I had opened years earlier when I was self-employed as a court reporter. When I did, I learned from my bank that it was possible to waive or forgive the taxes I would be required to pay because funds were withdrawn early—if I had my doctor write a letter declaring that I had no chance of surviving the disease. Despite my panic about the influx of medical bills, I refused to ask for a doctor's letter. I cried the whole time I was in the bank. In retrospect, I was making panicked, unreasonable decisions. I didn't understand then how much the trauma to my brain had changed me.

And then one day that stands out in my memory, when I was stretched out in my favorite reading chair with a book across my lap, I had an epiphany as clear and sudden as clouds parting to let the sun shine through. That grim statistic I read over and over again online? That average survival period of nine to fourteen months? That didn't have to be me. That *wasn't* me. I was not the statistical average.

Someone had to be the exception, the number that defied the statistic. Someone had to be the story with the happy ending. Why not me? I may someday die from brain cancer, but not today. It was my turning point, the instant in what eventually would be twenty-two months of treatment when I knew I would survive. "Attitude is everything," I told myself often. "What you let in is what you will be." It was a powerful moment, the moment in my journey when I stopped allowing fear to be the director of my life.

CHAPTER THIRTY

Italy!
April 2007

These days my imagination has the sun bending through leafy branches and sending shafts of light across fields of red tile roofs. The scents of fresh-baked pastries and cappuccino from the downstairs café waft through crisp morning air, blending with the poetic cadence of a foreign language that keeps time with the old gentleman's accordion music in the town's piazza. This dream has a name: Italy. I can't answer why that country moves me and stirs up images I want to paint with words like *illuminated* and *wind-blown* and *majestic*, or *color* and *light*, or even *romance*. I do know, however, that unlike the pleasure I derive from my daydream journeys—those types of journeys that are dependent upon my mind-set more than where I actually go—this anticipated journey is real.

These past two weeks I've devoured guidebooks, strategized with my two travel mates, Teri and Sharon, and canvassed stores for the best possible walking sandal known to womankind. I've booked airline tickets, created a calendar, altered that calendar, and more.

"Rome has some amazing American hotels you can use Starwood points for," Irwin says.

"Skip Siena and spend more nights in Florence," Carla says.

"Skip Florence and stay in Poggio Nardini just outside the city limits," Ann says. "It's easier to get around by car."

"Forget driving," Reed says. "Use the train."

I smile and let my friends offer advice. I graciously accept every book, every video, every suggestion they share. I know exactly where I want to go. I've done this trip so many times in my head I feel as if I've already gone.

"Skip the trip and save the money," Jack says.

I laugh. How to explain? I haven't even left home yet, but I already want to go again.

Three weeks later, standing barefoot in the sand that hugs Vernazza's picturesque harbor, I listen to the soft sound of waves lapping against boats moored at the dock. The silver chimes of the carillon bells from the hill above float through the sea-salt air. I'm in Italy. A short year ago I only imagined this. Tonight, a sense of peace fills me. I am grateful for family and friends, appreciative of this experience of a lifetime, and profoundly thankful for good health.

As I write this, ten years have passed since my brain tumor journey began. My brain scans remain stable, and my MRIs are now scheduled for every six months, a schedule that Dr. Chang tells me is the best it'll ever be. I'll take it. My hair grew back, though it's sparse and thin on the left side of my head due to the surgical scar and radiation damage. I'll take that too.

Three years after my surgery, I returned to work at Cal Poly, partly to complete the circle back to health, but mostly because I hoped that the fast-paced office environment would force brain function to improve. And while brain function did significantly improve, I've discovered a few neurological deficits—noticeable mostly to me—that remain today: occasional left–right confusion; a lack of sensation in my right hand that makes it hard to feel the keys on the keyboard; small quirks that occur when I am putting numbers in order; and, especially when I'm tired, a difficulty in finding and forming the right words to use in oral speech. I'll take those too.

I'd like to think that changes within me are profound, that I'm more soulful, more insightful about life matters, more tolerant of others' differences, more gentle and kind and patient and thoughtful. But the reality is that, at my core, I am who I was. And cancer has not changed that.

EPILOGUE

Another Tumor
May 2016

Time stops for no one. I celebrated ten years of good health in April of 2016, and on my drive to UCSF in May, I thought about asking Dr. Chang to relax the MRI schedule. In my mind, the conversation went something like this: "How about I push my MRIs to once a year? I mean, after all, it's been ten years. Do I *really* need to continue with the every-six-months MRIs?"

Before I could embarrass myself with that question, Dr. Chang walked into the patient waiting room on the eighth floor where I stood at the window overlooking Kezar Stadium and Golden Gate Park in San Francisco, the same spectacular view that calmed me each and every time these past ten years as I waited to hear my name called. "Are you here alone?" she asked. I was rarely alone. Jack was always with me, or Jen, or a friend. In ten years, I could only think of a handful of times I waited alone to hear MRI results. At my silent nod, she took my arm. "Let's go back," she said.

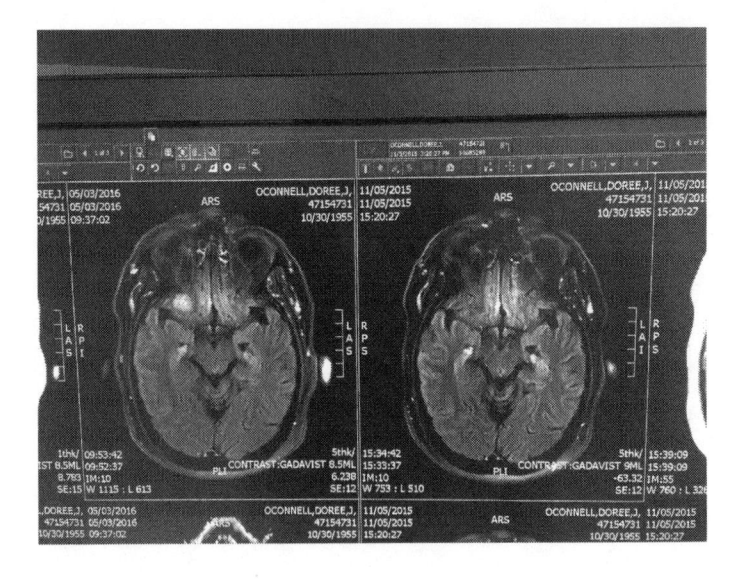

Dr. Berger told me in a phone call the next day how hard he had to look to see the new lesion. "It's small. But it's there. Very unusual to see a new tumor like yours ten years apart. First one was left parietal lobe, and the original surgical site remains unchanged. This new tumor is in the right frontal lobe. Different lobes and ten intervening years; it's not a recurrence. It's a new tumor. We don't know pathology yet, but with your history, we know what it is. Very unusual to see a second tumor," he repeated. "But then we know this disease is not in the least bit usual."

He paused. "Dr. Chang wants it out immediately. You already know your follow-up will be more radiation and oral chemo. But will you give me a week to explore your options? It may be that we can take care of this with a gamma knife procedure instead of traditional surgery. But I've got to take your case to the Tumor Board to hear what they have to say. And we will abide by their decision. But is it all right with you if we take a week?"

"I almost asked Dr. Chang if I could be done with the every-six-months MRIs," I blurted out.

"Ah," he said. "And now you see why we do that."

"Boy, was I ever cocky."

"Not cocky," he said. "Confident."

"I forgot to respect the disease."

"Not really. Every MRI you go to, every appointment you come to, you are respecting the disease. But GBM is sneaky, and it came back at you when you weren't looking. You are strong. And your attitude—" Dr. Berger paused. "I wish I could bottle up your attitude and spread it around to my other patients. You will get through this."

On May 24, 2016, I underwent a second craniotomy for a second brain tumor. No crisis situation as with the first surgery, no midnight ambulance ride, no tumor symptoms such as tripping up curbs or inability to hold a pen, no cognitive disabilities. If I hadn't seen the tumor on the MRI scans with my own two eyes, I'd seriously be questioning the need for surgery.

My medical team is in place, and I trust and respect them all. I'm in more studies than I can count, but I feel empowered to be asked to help. I'm home now, awaiting my marching orders from my radiologist and oncologist. I've done this before. I can do it again. Wish me luck.

THE FINAL CHAPTER

Today

> "These are the words I never wanted to
> write, you never wanted to hear,
> and I could not deliver..."

~~~

My mom completed her journey through brain cancer in San Luis Obispo, California, on July 18, 2018, more than twelve years after her initial diagnosis of GBM in April 2006. She got her decade—and then some. The words above are the opening words to the eulogy my dad wrote—and had his best friend read—for Doree's memorial service.

Although my mom's last few months were filled with doctor appointments, chemotherapy infusions, visits from physical and occupational therapists, and even a late-night emergency abdominal surgery, she never gave up, she never stopped smiling, and she never quit loving life. In her final weeks, friends and family gathered by her side, sharing pictures, stories, memories, and laughter. She died peacefully in her sleep. Doree's memorial service was held at a beautiful chapel in Los Osos, California, surrounded by the golden mountains known as the Seven Sisters, on California's Central Coast. Though we anticipated a good turnout at the service, we were shocked to find it was standing room only. But perhaps we shouldn't have been surprised: her fan club was, and still is, huge.

Doree's second brain tumor was detected in May 2016, ten years after her first, and was followed by surgery, radiation, and chemotherapy.

A third brain tumor, a recurrence of the second tumor, was discovered in September 2017. Her third surgery with Dr. Berger was successfully completed, followed by rounds of two new chemotherapy drugs and even more intense radiation. But alas, this tumor would not be stopped.

Doree lived twelve *full* years post-diagnosis, years "of family and friends, of joy and laughter, of life's bittersweet moments," as she so eloquently wrote in the introduction to this book. Throughout those years, she routinely received MRIs, followed by checkups and reviews from her team of doctors at UCSF, including a home visit in the spring of 2018 from her neuro-oncologist, Dr. Susan Chang. After more than a decade together, these two determined women, arms linked in battle, formed an extraordinary bond of friendship and mutual respect. It was Doree's hope that her participation in UCSF's cutting-edge medical research might one day help in the fight against GBM. And perhaps it already has, as the prognosis for GBM patients has improved by several months since Doree was diagnosed in 2006, thanks to the collective efforts of brain tumor researchers everywhere.

My mom had that character that is so rare to come by: pure warmth and grace. She was one of those kind, loving, and humble people whose demeanor instantly welcomes you in and makes you want to do great things. She was strong, brave, thoughtful, and, even to the end, uncomplaining and full of gratitude—a shining example to us all.

Doree wrote at the beginning of this book that what we are left with, at the end of our lives, are "our words, our actions, our memories, and the hope that—if we're lucky—our lives have mattered." Mom, your sixty-two years on this earth mattered. They were a gift to all of us. We love you forever, and we carry on in your absence, attempting to live each day in a way that would make you proud.

"Many people never get to meet the person they look up to most, but I was fortunate enough to be raised by mine."

Jennifer O'Connell
Closing words to my eulogy at Doree's memorial service
July 23, 2018

Made in the USA
Columbia, SC
08 May 2025